BEAD EMBROIDERY
JEWELRY PROJECTS

BEAD EMBROIDERY JEWELRY PROJECTS

Design and Construction, Ideas and Inspiration

Jamie Cloud Eakin

LARK JEWELRY & BEADING

LARK JEWELRY & BEADING

An Imprint of Sterling Publishing
387 Park Avenue South
New York, NY 10016

ISBN 978-1-4547-0815-5

Library of Congress Cataloging-in-Publication Data

Eakin, Jamie Cloud.
  Bead embroidery jewelry projects : design and construction, ideas and inspiration / Jamie Cloud Eakin.
    pages cm
  ISBN 978-1-4547-0815-5
  1. Beadwork. 2. Jewelry making. 3. Bead embroidery. I. Title.
  TT860.E245 2013
  745.594'2--dc23

Distributed in Canada by Sterling Publishing
c/o Canadian Manda Group, 165 Dufferin Street
Toronto, Ontario, Canada M6K 3H6
Distributed in the United Kingdom by GMC Distribution Services
Castle Place, 166 High Street, Lewes, East Sussex, England BN7 1XU
Distributed in Australia by Capricorn Link (Australia) Pty. Ltd.
P.O. Box 704, Windsor, NSW 2756, Australia

For information about custom editions, special sales, and premium and corporate purchases, please
contact Sterling Special Sales at 800-805-5489 or specialsales@sterlingpublishing.com.

Email academic@larkbooks.com for information about desk and examination copies.
The complete policy can be found at larkcrafts.com.

Manufactured in China

2 4 6 8 10 9 7 5 3 1

larkcrafts.com

Contents

18

23

26

28

31

34

38

41

46

52

57

62

69

74

80

86

93

97

101

110

113

115

118

120

122

128

131

133

136

139

Introduction

ONE OF THE PREMISES I LIVE BY IS "LIFE IS TOO SHORT TO WEAR ORDINARY JEWELRY," AND I'M SURE MANY OF YOU AGREE. Not only is it fun to wear your own creations, but there is also a satisfaction gained by making them that's difficult to achieve in many other areas of life. Perhaps that is why beading is so addictive.

There are many talents and skills used to create a piece of jewelry. So many decisions are made, from selecting the beads to choosing a color palette, that it can be challenging at times. This book focuses on the design and construction of bead-embroidered jewelry to address those challenges so you can be confident that the decisions you make will be successful. The projects are a fun way to learn, and they also offer ideas for your own special designs. So, even if you choose not to do a project, read through it. Each project was selected specifically to teach a lesson about design and construction and provide a format for you to use to create your own unique designs. Whether it's the sequence of the steps or the use of a particular technique, there are lessons you will find valuable on your own design journey.

And remember, there is an ancillary to my premise above: "Friends don't let friends wear ordinary jewelry." Enjoy!

Jamie

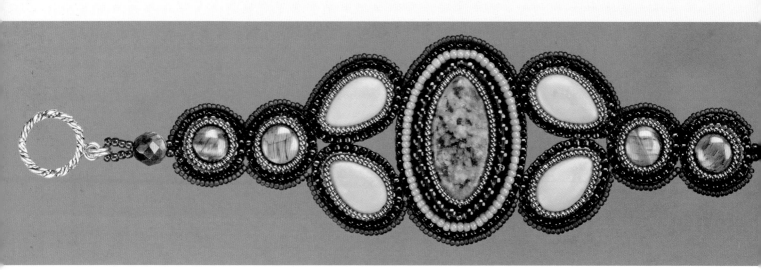

CHAPTER 1

Basics of Design and Construction

The purpose of this collection of projects is to advance your knowledge of design and construction for bead-embroidered jewelry.

Designing is "the what"—what shape, what colors, what components; in other words, what your finished piece is going to look like. After you've completed your design process, the construction phase begins. First you decide what to make, then you plan how to make it, and, finally, you execute your plan.

The projects are organized starting with simple designs and progressing to more complicated ones so you can build your knowledge and your confidence. I encourage you to read through each project (even if you choose not to create it) to gain an understanding of the process used, the sequence of steps, and the design considerations. Tips and lessons within a specific project may also apply to other projects in this book and your own original designs, so read everything for maximum benefit. The chapter titled Basic Procedures (page 143) includes procedures and processes used throughout the projects and can help you make design and construction decisions.

Design

The appeal of bead embroidery for most people is the ease of creating their own one-of-a-kind jewelry. Bead embroidery stitches are not complicated and mastering them isn't difficult, so taking the next step of creating your own designs is very seductive and is a step I encourage you to take. Although all creations are designs, "good designs" properly address color, shape, texture, balance/proportion/size/scale, and other issues.

Design is a formal discipline that can be studied through classes or books. The basic principles of design are used in this book as they apply specifically to bead embroidery and its unique attributes. Design is not the same as taste and style, which are unique to a person and involve individual preference, but taste and style are critically important when you progress to the stage of being a designer. Developing your taste and style involves imagining possibilities and deciding what you want to do. The exercises that follow will help you imagine and develop your unique style.

EXERCISE 1

Really look at things. For example, look at a necklace you like and take the time to evaluate exactly what pleases you. Is it the colors? The shape? Look at the entire necklace and break it down into pieces. Is it the particular beads that were used or the way the pendant hangs? The objective is to educate yourself in a fundamental way.

EXERCISE 2

Spend time looking at designs you don't like. Turn off the voice that says, "If you can't say anything nice, don't say anything at all." An important part of your education is to explore the negative. What exactly is wrong with the necklace? Take time to remake it in your mind. What changes would you make that could turn the necklace into one that you liked?

EXERCISE 3

When you find something you like, reduce it to a simple line drawing (see photo 1 and figure 1). Re-arrange, alter, or otherwise make changes to that drawing for a similar but different design (figure 2). And finally, create a new design as in photo 2.

The two necklaces in this exercise are entirely different, but you can now see how one evolved from the other. You can use this process to create your own unique designs.

EXERCISE 4

Become aware of what inspires you. Make a note of those things and let them invade your consciousness. Keep an inspiration book—write notes, paste pictures, or make drawings in it. Inspirations can come from anywhere: a piece of jewelry, a bead or cabochon, a beautiful outfit or painting, or a technique you want to learn and explore. Your book can help you get inspired and stay that way.

If you get into the habit of doing the things in these exercises, then creating your own designs will become easier and more successful.

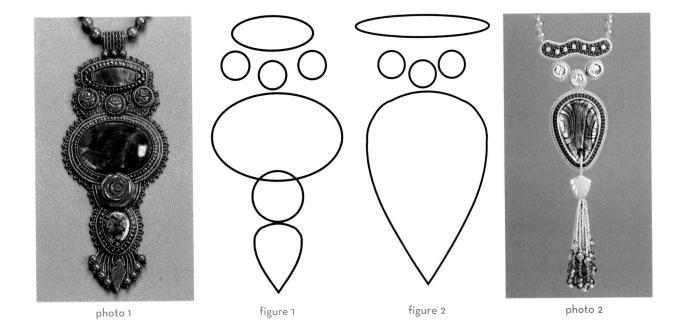

photo 1   figure 1   figure 2   photo 2

Construction

Construction is the how-to of putting together bead embroidery stitches and techniques to create a piece of jewelry. The Techniques Index on page 148 shows the stitches and techniques used in the projects. The index is both a reference and a communication tool because in beading the same stitch is often known by many different names. The projects in this book assume knowledge of the stitches and techniques. If there is a technique used that you are not familiar with, feel free to substitute with another that you know and create your own unique design.

A critical part of success in creating jewelry concerns the quality of the construction. Here are a few things to keep in mind:

- Use quality beads, findings, and other materials.
- Common sense is important in bead embroidery. Use it to determine how many times to stitch and reinforce beadwork.
- Try on creations often while constructing. Gravity and body shape have a significant impact on jewelry, and that can't be seen working on a flat table.
- Glue is a tool only used to position components before stitching. Glue will fail. Beadwork, however, has been shown to last at least a hundred years. When glue fails, make sure the beadwork prevents the glued item from falling off, getting lost, or breaking. It can then be re-secured with glue if desired.

Design Tools

Design tools help you create a successful design and also assist in the construction process. The tools that follow are for necklaces; see page 127 for tools for bracelets.

NECK FORMS AND COLLAR FORMS

One of the most useful tools to add to your beading kit is a neck form. The best is a full-size, full-body mannequin used by people who sew, a "dressmaker dummy." However, this can be an expensive tool, and there is also the problem of storage. A great alternative is to use a neck form made to display necklaces. Select a three-dimensional display that is at least 12 inches (30.5 cm) tall and covered in either fabric or leather. A fabric or leather covering allows you to pin your beadwork on the display if desired. Although the display neck is a useful alternative, keep in mind as you design that its neck size is usually smaller than actual necks. You'll need to compensate for this in your designs.

Another alternative that is easy, inexpensive, and useful is a flat form made on a piece of paper—a Neck Form Page. You can use this as you design and bead, and it is easy to create.

Making a Neck Circle and Neck Form Page

1 Take a piece of string and wrap it around your neck, positioning it at the base of your neck, not where a dog-collar-type choker would go. Cut the string to match your neck size.

2 Now arrange the string into a circle with the ends just touching in the center of a piece of paper. Keep the string as round as possible. Use a dark pen and trace under it. If you are having trouble creating a circle, get a large canned good from the kitchen, trace that circle on the paper, and use it to help arrange and trace the string.

3 Hold the paper up to a light and fold it in half, matching the lines as much as possible. Fold in half again (so the circle is now in quarters), again matching up the lines.

4 Leave the paper folded and cut it out on the lines to create a circle that represents your neck size. Mark the fold lines. This is the Neck Circle.

5 Take a new piece of paper and fold it in half, then in half again, making another quarter page. Mark the fold lines with ink. Take the circle cut out in step 4 and place it in the center of the paper, matching up the fold lines on both. Trace around the circle form. This is your Neck Form Page.

6 Keep both the Neck Circle and the Neck Form Page in your beading tool kit to use when you are creating a design. These will be used in many of the projects that follow.

Use the Neck Circle and Neck Form Page when designing a necklace. They will give you a good perspective on size and are useful to draw on and record design decisions. The key is to remember that this is a flat form, but a neck is not flat.

 tip You can create large, medium, and small neck forms, which are useful when you are making jewelry for someone else. For small, use a string length of 15 inches (38.1 cm); for large, use 18 to 19 inches (45.7 to 48.3 cm).

If your neck and shoulders were shaped like figure 1, the flat circle would work perfectly. In reality, necks flow in a gradual slope into the shoulders, as in figure 2. This slope will affect how your necklace will lie on the body, and you need to account for that in your design and construction.

figure 1   figure 2

Making a Collar Form

You can easily create a form to make a pattern for a beaded collar using the Neck Circle.

1 Get a piece of paper large enough to accommodate the design for your beaded collar. Fold it in half vertically and mark the center line.

2 Match up the center line on your Neck Circle and the paper folded in step 1, and trace the Neck Circle onto the paper.

3 Draw marks ½ inch (1.3 cm) from the Neck Circle on the front and sides. Make a mark 1 inch (2.5 cm) from the back neck. Draw a line centered at the 1-inch (2.5 cm) mark that is 3½ inches (8.9 cm) long; the line is 1¾ inches (4.4 cm) long on each side of the center 1-inch (2.5 cm) mark (figure 3). Connect that line to the other marks, circling the neck. Mark 1 inch (2.5 cm) down from the back of the neck on each side (figure 4).

This delineates the inner neck portion of the Collar Form. It is larger than the Neck Circle in the front and on the sides to accommodate edge beading and provide comfort and ease. It is shorter in the back to provide room for edge beads and clasps. The shape is not a true circle so that when the back portion is joined, it will create a cone shape.

Once the inner neck is completed you can draw the area around it to create the beading area of the collar (figure 5). Fold it in half lengthwise and cut so that each side matches (figure 6).

tip Always create a pattern out of paper and try it on before tracing it onto the under-backing and doing any beadwork. Check the size and shape before you spend hours beading!

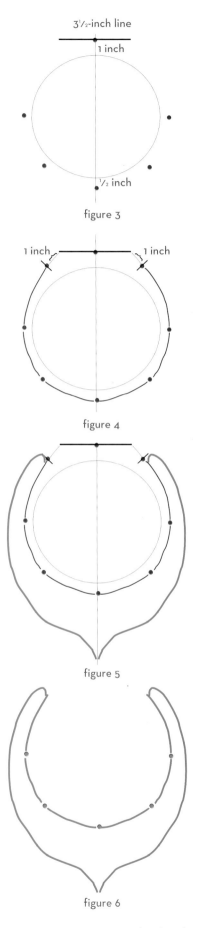

3½-inch line

1 inch

½ inch

figure 3

1 inch   1 inch

figure 4

figure 5

figure 6

SUBSTITUTIONS

Feel free to substitute bead sizes 15° with 14°, 8° with 9°, and 6° with 5°.

The bead sizes used for the base row of a Standard/Plain Bezel are based on the profile of the cabochon used to make the project. Refer to Standard/Plain Bezel on page 150 and substitute the size of the base row beads as needed.

BEADING KIT

All projects include the size of backing and outer-backing needed in the supplies list. Unless noted otherwise, the backing material used in the projects was Lacy's Stiff Stuff (available at most bead stores and suppliers). Other recommended backings include thick fused interfacing (available at fabric stores) and starched felt (available in the children's section of craft stores). Ultrasuede was used as the outer-backing material in the projects. Other materials that can be used for outer-backing include any fused fabrics.

Standard Beading Kit

Lacy's Stiff Stuff is available only in white, but it can be dyed or colored with permanent markers. The best color to use for the outer-backing is a color to match the thread used for the edge stitching.

Size 12 beading needles
Beading thread (Nymo, Silamide, SoNo, or other as desired)
Glue
Scissors
Paper and pen

 tip Consider having an assortment of beading needle sizes on hand to use depending on the task. Size 12 needles work wonderfully for all stitches and techniques. Larger needles, such as a size 10, are easier to thread, and they are thicker, so they're easier to handle. The larger needles work well for certain stitches such as Picot Stitch, Sunshine Edge, Clean Edge, and any other stitch that does not require multiple stitches through beads.

STANDARD NECKLACE KITS

There are two standard necklace kits used in the beaded necklace projects in this book, and each includes a head pin. String a couple of beads used in the necklace onto the head pin, and trim and loop it on the end of the chain for a professional finish.

Many of the necklace projects are completed by stringing beads for the necklace strand. Beaded ropes are great substitutes for bead strands and work wonderfully with bead-embroidered pieces; feel free to substitute here as well.

The instructions for creating the bead strands include how to create beaded loops at the ends of the strands. The loops are used to attach purchased findings using two jump rings on each end. This methodology allows for maximum flexibility. Broken findings can be easily replaced. The type of closure, the color, and the size can be changed at any time.

Standard Necklace Kit Using Thread

Two 6° seed beads

Eighteen to twenty-two 11° seed beads

1 hook

4-inch (10.2 cm) length of chain, links at least 4 mm in diameter

4 jump rings, 5 mm

1 head pin, 2 inches (5.1 cm)

Pliers

Wire cutters

 tip A useful necklace closure is a hook on one side and a length of chain on the other. This provides for easy adjustment of the necklace's length for other people with a different neck size or for personal preferences. This is helpful when changing clothing from an open neckline to a turtleneck, making it easy to adjust where the necklace hangs.

Standard Necklace Kit Using Flexible Beading Wire

Two 6° seed beads

Eighteen to twenty-two 11° seed beads

1 hook

4-inch (10.2 cm) length of chain, links at least 4 mm in diameter

4 jump rings, 5 mm

1 head pin, 2 inches (5.1 cm)

20 inches (50.8 cm) of flexible beading wire, 0.019 diameter

2 crimp beads

2 crimp covers, optional

Pliers

Wire cutters

Crimping pliers

tip Don't use color-lined, silver-lined, or coated beads for the seed bead loops at the end of the necklace strand. There is a lot of friction on these beads, which will rub off linings and coatings. Use an 11° bead that matches the 6° bead. Even if those seed beads are not used anywhere else, they still coordinate as an end loop.

CHAPTER 2

The One Necklaces

The design journey starts with "the one," a single focal that is the star of the show. There's a beautiful simplicity to a single focal embraced by bead embroidery. This type of design is wonderful because it's so versatile. Whether it's for office wear or a gift for a friend with conservative tastes, these designs are ultimately wearable. Designs of "the one" are perfect for learning bead embroidery or trying new techniques. There's nothing like actually doing a stitch to perfect your skills.

The One: Pendants

The most popular use for a single focal is a pendant-style necklace. Most beaders start designing using a fancy focal (bead, cabochon, donut, or other component) that is elaborate, beautiful, and the source of inspiration. You saw it, you had to buy it, and now you want to bead it. In this situation, the beading provides a frame to highlight and accentuate the magnificence of the focal. The selection of colors for the seed beads is usually driven by the focal's colors, and simple techniques are selected so they don't fight with its pattern. Instead, beadwork frames the focal to be the star.

These are the design steps for a pendant necklace:

1 Select a focal and assemble a pile of beads you might use in the design, including seed beads and larger beads for the necklace strand.

2 From the pile, select the beads to use for the necklace. Choose colors of seed beads based on the colors in the neck- lace beads and the focal. Pick the seed bead sizes for the base and bezel rows depending on the profile of the focal.

3 Select a bezel technique, an edge technique, and an attachment technique, and plan your design.

4 Review your design. You may want to change your selection of beads based on the techniques you plan to use.

5 Record your design plan with notes or photos.

6 You now have your design and are ready to enter the construction phase.

The Purple Impressions Necklace (page 18) was designed based on these six steps. First, the cabochon was selected. Strands and beads that included all of the colors in the cabochon were assembled into the "possible materials" pile. The next step was to select a strand to use in the necklace. There is not a right and wrong here. This project used one of the purple strands, but it could have used the other purple one or even the beige (see photo, below). Select the strand first, because that selection will influence the selection of seed bead colors.

tip

Good designs have balance and proportion. Remember those principles when selecting the beads for the necklace strand. Pendants, bib, and totem styles with a large profile require at least an 8-mm bead (if not larger) for the necklace strands. Puffed flat beads (round, oval, rectangular) are good choices for these designs. The necklace section, whether a bead strand or a rope, needs to be in proper proportion to the beadwork it is supporting. Too often beaders are so focused on the embroidered section of the design that they neglect the design as a whole. Get in touch with your "inner stringer" and design the necklace section with the same enthusiasm as the bead-embroidered section.

It is important to first select the beads for the necklace strand. Many times beaders select the seed beads and stitch up the focal. Later they try to finish the necklace or bracelet and can't find the right color of beads to use for stringing because they are locked into a color palette. The beadwork remains an unfinished object—a UFO. If you select the beads to use for stringing the necklace strand first, seed bead colors can be selected for a total design that really works.

A key part of designing is deciding which colors to use for the beadwork. The primary color in the focal was used in the Purple Impressions Necklace (below, left). The secondary color was used in the I'm a Fan Necklace (below, middle), and an accent color was used in the Slice of Heaven Necklace (below, right). All of these approaches work.

Deciding which color(s) to use for the beadwork is often a matter of personal choice or taste, but it may be influenced by other factors. An example of this is the Nature's Essence Necklace (page 22): this focal has many shades of green. If one of those greens was selected for the rest of the beadwork, then that green would dominate, and the other green shades would get lost. To make the jewelry wearable with all of the greens in the focal, the secondary color (brown) was selected to create the necklace.

tip

Use your closet and the colors inside to help with your design choices. Use the predominant colors in your closet as the secondary or accent colors in your designs for maximum wearability. Don't make a black necklace to wear on a black sweater, because you won't be able to see it easily!

Focals that are plain, solid colors are usually easy to find and provide excellent design opportunities. A plain focal doesn't mean a plain design! This is exemplified by the Summer Flower Necklace (page 23), which uses one of the plainest focals of all: a solid white cabochon. Inspiration for designs can be driven by a strand of necklace beads or the selection of a fancy technique. Pairing these with a solid-color focal is a great way to create a design. In this case, however, the design steps aren't always done in a strict order. The motivation and inspiration for your design may start, for example, at step 3, with a desire to learn and use a particular bezel technique. Keep that in your plan and simply go back afterward and fill in from step 1.

tip

Plain, solid-color focals are also the easiest way to create designs to wear with wardrobes that include patterns and prints. Jewelry designs for those wardrobes work best when they are monochromatic and bold, like the Orange Options Necklace (page 22).

The One: Going Beyond

Using one center focal with a few bead rows is a great look, but you can also add embellishments of other beads and stitch techniques for even more intricate and stunning looks. Use the same design steps on page 16, except in step 2, include other bead sizes and shapes. The plan will be more complex and step 3 may include many techniques for the surface stitching.

Purple
Impressions
Necklace

What You Need

1 purple impression jasper designer-cut cabochon, 52 x 34 mm

32 quartz round beads, purple (dyed), 8 mm

8 riverstone round beads, 6 mm

16 metal rondelles, antique gold, 4 mm

5 glass round beads, metallic gold, 3 mm

1 piece each of backing and outer-backing, 3 x 3½ inches (7.6 x 8.9 cm)

Standard Necklace Kit Using Flexible Beading Wire (page 15)

Standard Beading Kit (page 14)

Seed Beads

  2 grams of 15° gold metallic

  2 grams of 15° purple color-lined

  3 grams of 11° purple color-lined

  1 gram of 11° gold metallic

What You Do

1 Glue the cabochon onto the backing and let it dry. Create a Standard/Plain Bezel with the 11° purple seed beads for the base row and the 15° gold metallic beads for the bezel row.

2 Trim the backing. Apply the outer-backing and trim it. Stitch a Sunshine Edge row with the 11° purple beads. Find and mark the center top and bottom.

3 Stitch a Herringbone Loop Attachment 11 beads tall at the center top using the 11° purple beads.

> **tip** Use a short strand of beading wire to design the necklace strand early in the beading process. If you are creating a rope to use for the necklace, make 2 to 3 inches (5.1 to 7.6 cm) of the rope. Keep this strand design with the beadwork to help make design decisions as you bead. Use it to determine the length of the bail.

4 For the final edge technique, use the Wave Edge with the 11° gold beads for the lift and the 15° purple seed beads for the outside row. (See tip below.)

> **tip** When creating an edge that has a set number of base beads, start from the top and create each side simultaneously. When you approach the bottom, count the remaining base beads to see if the stitch will work out evenly. If it does, continue and meet in the middle. If it does not, create a variation that you like. In the photo right, 3-mm gold beads were used to create an interesting design variation along the bottom.

5 Create the necklace using the Standard Necklace Instructions for Flexible Beading Wire (page 145) with the pattern, right (figure 1). Use the 8-mm and 6-mm rounds, 4-mm rondelles, and 11° gold seed beads.

> **tip** The 11° gold seed beads between the larger beads add flexibility to the necklace and design flair.

figure 1

I'm a Fan Necklace

Based on Purple Impressions Necklace (page 18)

Key Elements: Red creek jasper fan component,
50 x 10 mm; tiger jasper round beads, 4 mm

Necklace Strand: Tiger jasper round beads, 8 mm and
4 mm; metal rondelles, antique gold, 4 mm; Standard
Necklace Instructions for Flexible Beading Wire (page 145)

Stitches/Techniques: Standard/Plain Bezel using Couch
Stitch with 4-mm beads for the base row, Sunshine Edge,
Pointed Edge, Square Stitch Bail

tip

Look at everything in the bead store and
beyond—chances are you can use it in bead
embroidery! The center stone in this necklace
is part of a gemstone fan set purchased at a
discount because one of the parts of the fan
was broken. Take advantage of those bargains
because parts of the fan can be used individu-
ally, and the broken part tossed.

lesson

Using Couch Stitch

Rows of Backstitch and rows
of Couch Stitch will end up
looking the same: a row of
beads. A 6° seed bead is
approximately the same size
as a 4-mm round, but seed
beads have differences in their
width; some are skinny, others
are fatter. Therefore, you can
use Backstitch and know there
will be beads to create a proper fit. However,
there isn't a differential with a 4-mm round bead.
Therefore, use the Couch Stitch to plan and
manage the fit.

figure 1

Using Couch Stitch with a round or an oval focal
involves picking up all the beads at once to sur-
round the focal, then adding or removing beads
to adjust the fit. However, when focals have corners, it is easier to place the beads in sections
to create the fit. For this project, the edge was
segmented and stitched as follows (figure 1): red
first, orange second, pink next, and yellow last.
This approach is not only easier to fit, but it also
provides for better symmetry.

Slice of Heaven Necklace

Based on Purple Impressions Necklace (page 18)

Key Elements: Agate triangle-shaped polished slice, 55 x 35 mm; crystal bicone beads, crystal copper, 3 mm

Necklace Strand: Brecciated jasper round beads, 8 mm; crystal bicone beads, crystal copper, 3 mm; Standard Necklace Instructions for Flexible Beading Wire (page 145)

Stitches/Techniques: Standard/Plain Bezel, Bead-Across Bezel, Sunshine Edge, Rope Edge, Side Petal Edge, Herringbone Loop Attachment

tip Beading around corners often exposes the beading thread. Hide the thread by adding some smaller beads into the row. First stitch the row, and then travel around the row through all the beads at least once. Now travel around the row again, adding smaller beads in the corner spaces as pictured below. For a row using 6° beads, add 11° beads. For a row using 11° beads, add 15° beads.

tip This is a designer-cut focal; in other words, there is no symmetry. In these cases, gravity will dominate the design. Estimate which edge beads to use for the bail and test it by stitching a piece of thread in the selected edge beads

and letting it hang to see how gravity affects the design. If the way the piece hangs is not what you want, select different edge beads until you get the effect you desire. You can either select the center beads and accept how it hangs, or select edge beads off from the center that make the pendant hang as you want. This project uses beads off center so that the point of the triangle hangs in a particular way.

Nature's Essence Necklace

Based on Purple Impressions Necklace (page 18)

Key Element: Green impression jasper designer-cut cabochon, 41 x 26 mm

Necklace Strand: Bronzite round beads, 8 mm; Standard Necklace Instructions for Direct Attachment Clean Edge (page 146)

Stitches/Techniques: Standard/Plain Bezel, Clean Edge

tip Use thread to alter the color of transparent beads and create your own unique bead color. As a general rule, a light-color thread is used with transparent beads to prevent a color change. However, you can also take advantage of this phenomenon. Select a transparent bead that is close to the color you want to end up with, then select a thread color to alter it. This necklace was stitched with a dark brown thread to darken the color. The thread color shows through and changes the appearance of the beads.

Orange Options Necklace

Based on Purple Impressions Necklace (page 18)

Key Elements: Ocean jasper puffed flat rectangle bead, 28 x 24 mm; freshwater pearl beads, orange, 7 mm; crystal bicone beads, topaz, 3 mm

Necklace Strand: Freshwater pearl beads, orange, 7 mm; Standard Necklace Instructions for Flexible Beading Wire (page 145)

Stitches/Techniques: Standard/Plain Bezel, Clover Stitch, Sunshine Edge, Side Petal Edge, Double Herringbone Loop Attachment—Sideways Loop Variation

tip Use some beads from the necklace strand within the surface beadwork to create unity in the design.

Summer
Flower
Necklace

What You Need

1 white aventurine cabochon, 40 x 30 mm

16 millefiori puffed flat oval beads, aqua/green/white, 10 x 14 mm

2 millefiori oval beads, aqua/green/white, 6 x 8 mm

18 glass pearl round beads, white, 6 mm

2 fire-polished round beads, light aqua, 3 mm

8 to 10 crystal bicone beads, light azore, 3 mm

8 to 10 crystal bicone beads, chrysolite, 3 mm

1 crystal bicone bead, chrysolite, 4 mm

1 piece each of backing and outer-backing, 2½ x 2½ inches (6.4 x 6.4 cm)

Standard Necklace Kit Using Thread (page 15)

Standard Beading Kit (page 14)

Seed Beads

1 gram of 15° white ceylon

3 grams of 11° white ceylon

1 gram of 11° pale green color-lined

1 gram of 11° light aqua color-lined

1 gram of 8° light blue AB

What You Do

1 Mark the backing with center lines horizontally and vertically to assist in the strategic placement of beads in the bezel. Glue the cabochon to the center and let it dry.

> **tip** It is a good idea to mark a vertical center line and one or more horizontal lines on the backing even if your plan does not require it . . . especially if you are in the habit of changing your mind!

2 The bezel is a combination of the Bead-Across Bezel and the Flower Bezel. Stitch a base row with the 11° white beads. Stitch one 3-mm fire-polished bead at the center top and one at the bottom. Now add a flower on the center of each side using the 11° light aqua for the flower, the 8° for the center, and the 15° beads at the top. Add a flower above and below the flowers on each side using the 11° pale green for the flower and the 8° for the center, topped with the 15° beads. Complete the bezel row by filling in with the 15° beads. Stitch an additional row using the 11° white beads.

3 Trim the backing. Apply the outer-backing and trim it. Stitch a Sunshine Edge row with the 11° white beads. Find and mark the center top and bottom.

4 Stitch an Added Bead Attachment with one 15°, two 11° white on the sides, and the 4-mm bicone at the center top. See figure 1 for the appropriate layout, depending on whether the center is one bead or two.

figure 1

5 Finish the edge with the Side Petal Edge using the 15°, 11° white, and 3-mm bicone beads, alternating the two colors of the bicones. Start at the top on each side and meet at the bottom. Adjust the edge stitch as needed to meet at the center bottom.

6 String the necklace with the glass pearls and millefiori beads using the Standard Necklace Instructions for Thread (page 144). Add the oval millefiori bead at the center and stitch through the 4-mm bicone in the Added Bead Attachment (figure 2).

figure2

Rose Garden Necklace

Based on Summer Flower Necklace (page 23)

Key Elements: Amazonite flat round bead, 40 mm; new jade carved rose bead, 20 mm; glass leaf beads, light aqua/brown, 10 x 18 mm; crystal bicone beads, topaz, 3 mm

Necklace Strand: Amazonite round beads, 8 mm; crystal bicone beads, topaz, 6 mm; Standard Necklace Instructions for Flexible Beading Wire (page 145)

Stitches/Techniques: Standard/Plain Bezel, Double Herringbone Loop Attachment—Sideways Loop Variation, Sunshine Edge, Side Petal Edge

tip

Stitching beads on top of beads can be done simply for design purposes or to hide defects in beads. This is very useful when you notice a problem with a focal. Sometimes an off coloration in a stone or some other flaw becomes obvious after it's framed with beads, and stitching beads on top of it is a great way to hide these flaws. This is also perfect for hiding holes drilled into pendants that have been repurposed as a bead-embroidered focal.

Super
Simplicity
Necklace

What You Need

1 lampwork glass cabochon by Pam Killingsworth, 49 x 32 mm

1 glue-on metal bail, nickel plated, 15 x 9 mm

18-inch (45.7 cm) silver chain with clasp

1 piece each of backing and outer-backing, 2¹⁄₂ x 2 inches (6.4 x 5.1 cm)

1 piece of flashing, 2¹⁄₂ x 2 inches (6.4 x 5.1 cm)

Standard Beading Kit (page 14)

Seed Beads

1 gram of 15° silver luster

2 grams of 11° capri blue color-lined

What You Do

1 Glue the cabochon onto the backing and let it dry. Create a Standard/Plain Bezel with the 11° beads for the base row and the 15° beads for the bezel row.

2 Trim the backing. Place the piece on the flashing and trace around it. Trim the flashing to approximately ¼ inch (6 mm) inside the traced line. Measure against the beaded piece and make sure there is enough blank edge for the placement of edge stitches; trim more if needed. Glue the flashing to the back of the beadwork and let it dry.

3 Glue the metal bail to the flashing. (Be sure to use a glue that dries flexible.) Once the glue is dry, stitch the bail to the beadwork. Position this stitch above the flashing and as far down from the edge as will fit. Check by sticking a needle through the backing and look at the front side. A good position is inside the last beaded row (in this case, the base row). Stitch from the back side, wrapping the thread around the bail, and while on the front, stitch between the base and the bezel row. If there was an additional row, the stitch on the front would be between the additional row and the base row. Using doubled thread, stitch around the bail three times and tie a square knot. Trim away from the knot and glue the ends down (photo 1).

photo 1

4 Apply the outer-backing. See the Tip below to avoid problems trimming the outer-backing when a bail is in the way.

> **tip** Use the profile of the cabochon bottom to trim the outer-backing, then turn it and put the trimmed area on top for gluing.

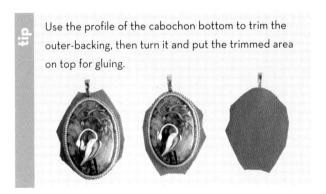

5 Once the glue is dry, trim the rest of the outer-backing. Use the Clean Edge with the 11° beads to stitch the final row. Start in the middle of one of the sides to more easily manage bead placement near the bail.

6 Insert the chain through the bail.

Loop-de-Loop Necklace

What You Need

1 red creek jasper puffed flat oval bead, 35 x 25 mm

28 olive jade round beads, 8 mm

8 carnelian agate faceted round beads, 8 mm

18 metal rondelles, antique gold, 4 mm

1 piece each of backing (dark green starched felt) and outer-backing, each 5 x 5 inches (12.7 x 12.7 cm) (see Note)

Standard Necklace Kit Using Thread (page 15)

Standard Beading Kit (page 14)

Note: The technique used for this necklace leaves some backing surface uncovered. If the necklace is held in certain ways, the backing can be seen, but it can't be seen when worn. Use a backing that looks acceptable when uncovered, such as a colored starched felt.

Seed Beads

1 gram of 15° pale olive luster

2 grams of 11° rust color-lined luster

2 grams of 11° dark gold color-lined

4 grams of 11° light gold color-lined

6 grams of 11° pale olive color-lined

8 grams of 11° olive opaque

1 gram of 11° amber transparent

1 gram of 6° copper metallic matte

What You Do

1 Mark the backing with a vertical center line. Mark a horizontal line 1 inch (2.5 cm) down from the top. Mark additional lines under it spaced 3/16 inch (5 mm) apart. Glue the bead centered on the vertical line 1 inch (2.5 cm) from the top and let it dry (figure 1). Sew the bead on with the One-Bead Stitch.

figure 1

2 Create a Standard/Plain Bezel with the 6° beads for the base row and the 15° beads for the bezel row.

3 Use the 11° rust beads and the Picot Stitch to stitch around the base row starting at the second line down (figure 2). Repeat for another row. Stitch around again, but this time with a Loop Stitch of seven beads using the dark gold 11° beads (figure 3).

figure 2   figure 3

4 Use the Loop Stitch and create loops on the second line down to the right of the beadwork. Start in the center and stitch two loops each using 13 light gold seed beads, then 17 pale olive seed beads, and ending with 21 olive seed beads.

figure 4

5 Measure the distance from the center to the outside of the loops just created (figure 4). Mark that measurement on the lines below, stopping at the end of the beaded section. Use those markings and draw the border for the beadwork, estimating the section below the beadwork (figure 5).

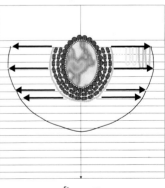

figure 5

6 Repeat step 4 on the left side. Stitch a row on top, using the rust beads and Backstitch (figure 6). Trim the top and cut on the line drawn, as illustrated in figure 7.

7 Fill each line with loops as described in step 4. Adjust the colors as needed for the bottom area (figure 8).

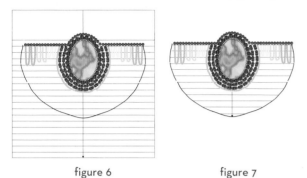

figure 6   figure 7

8 Apply the outer-backing and trim. Stitch the edge with the Clean Edge stitch, using the 11° rust beads across the top, and the olive beads below.

figure 8

> **tip**
>
> When fitting beads into a defined area, change the normal stitching sequence to force any fit adjustments into the least obvious area. For this project, start at one edge of the line. As you approach the other edge, when there are three more loops to go, skip to the end and stitch the last loop. Then fill in the remaining two loops. The spacing works well in figure 9 below. There is too much room in figure 10, so spread the spacing on these final two loops. There is a shortage of room in figure 11, so share a bead on one of the loops.
>
>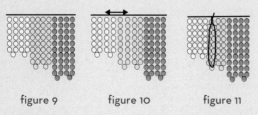
>
> figure 9   figure 10   figure 11

9 Create the necklace portion using the Standard Necklace Instructions for Direct Attachment Clean Edge (page 146). Use the pattern as illustrated with the 8-mm round beads, the 4-mm rondelles, and the olive, rust, and amber 11° beads (figure 12).

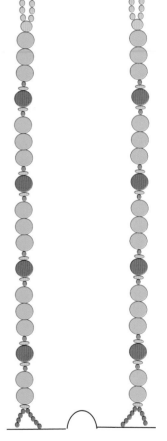

figure 12

Morning
Dew
Necklace

What You Need

1 mother-of-pearl carved flower, 48 x 55 mm

36 freshwater pearls, silver, 9 mm

36-inch (91.4 cm) strand of blue lace agate chip beads, medium size

1 piece each of backing and outer-backing, 3½ x 3 inches (8.9 x 7.6 cm)

Standard Necklace Kit Using Thread (page 15)

Standard Beading Kit (page 14)

Seed Beads

2 grams of 15° light blue luster

20 grams of 11° light blue opaque

2 grams of 6° silver pearl

> **tip**
> Chips are an economical way to collect a particular stone and cost less than beads or cabochons of the same stone. If you have a limited budget but want a particular stone, look for chips in that stone to use in your designs. (I even have some emerald and diamond chips in my stash!)

What You Do

1 If needed, create a flat base for the mother-of-pearl flower (see the lesson Create a Flat Base, page 119). Glue it onto the backing and let it dry.

2 Create a Standard/Plain Bezel using the 6° beads for the base row and the 15° beads for the bezel row. Stitch an additional row with the 11° beads. Trim the backing. Apply the outer-backing and trim it. Stitch the edge row with the 11° beads using the Sunshine Edge. Find and mark the center top and bottom.

3 Create a Double Herringbone Loop Attachment—Sideways Loop Variation using the 11° beads at the center top.

> **tip**
> Stitch the bail on before adding fringe. This gives you a smaller piece of beadwork to handle, so it is easier. And thread won't get tangled into fringe that isn't there yet!

4 Read the lesson Chip Loop Fringe to the right, and create the fringe based on those instructions. Start with six chips on the first side, a center bottom chip, and five chips on the other side. Stitch the center loop and the next two loops on each side using the same length.

Reduce the bead count by one for subsequent loops. Do a total of 21 loops.

5 Use the Pointed Edge to finish the edge area between the fringe and bail using the 11° beads as the base and the 15° bead as the center top of the point.

6 Create the necklace using the Standard Necklace Instructions for Thread (page 144). Alternate the 9-mm pearls with an 11° bead for the strand design.

> **lesson**
>
> ### Chip Loop Fringe
>
> **1** Use doubled thread and start in the center of the area to be fringed.
>
> **2** Pick up five seeds and one chip. Repeat until you have the length you desire. This last chip is the bottom of the fringe. Substitute with another type or shape of bead as desired for the bottom.
>
> **3** For the other side of the loop, start with eight seeds, then one chip. This will position the chips on this side of the strand in between the chips on the first side. Pick up five seeds and one chip until you have one less chip than on the first side. Fill to the top with seed beads so that the bottom chip/bead is at the center, generally seven to nine beads. Figures 1 and 2 are examples of a center loop. Use figure 1 when the center is two edge beads, and figure 2 when the center is one bead.
>
>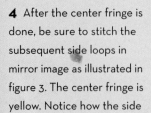
>
> figure 1   figure 2
>
> **4** After the center fringe is done, be sure to stitch the subsequent side loops in mirror image as illustrated in figure 3. The center fringe is yellow. Notice how the side loops (orange and blue) are mirror images of each other.
>
>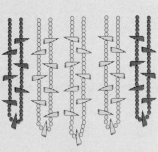
>
> figure 3
>
> **5** For U-shaped fringe, make the center loop plus one or two loops on each side of it the same length. Reduce the bead count on subsequent loops.
>
> **6** For V-shaped fringe, make the center loop and then reduce the bead count on each subsequent loop.
>
> *Lesson continued on next page*

7 To shorten the fringes, reduce the bead count from the bottom, not the top as you do with typical fringe techniques. You need at least five seed beads between the edge and the nearest chip for the fringe to hang properly, so reduce the count of seed beads from the bottom, usually one or two beads. When the elimination gets to a chip, estimate the seed bead equivalent of the space used by the chip (usually two) and adjust as needed. See figure 4. Remember to adjust the bead count on one side of the loop when fringing a curved edge (see tip below).

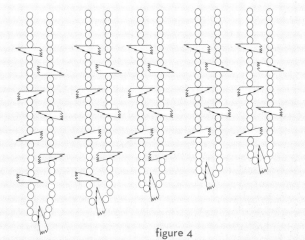

figure 4

project Variation

Ruby Curve Necklace

Based on Morning Dew Necklace (page 31)
Key Elements: Ruby in fuschite puffed flat round bead, 30 mm; 20-inch (50.8 cm) strand of cranberry aventurine chip beads
Necklace Strand: Aventurine round beads, teal green, 8 mm; Malaysian jade faceted round beads, berry (dyed), 10 mm; metal rondelles, bright gold, 5 mm; Standard Necklace Instructions for Flexible Beading Wire (page 145)
Stitches/Techniques: Standard/Plain Bezel, Sunshine Edge, Square Stitch Bail, Curves, Bugles, and the Lazy Stitch Lesson (page 125), Fringe Edge—Loop Fringe

The loop fringe's bottom sequence is one gold 11°, one chip, one teal 11°, one chip, one teal 11°, one chip, one teal 11°, one chip, one teal 11°, one chip, one gold 11°. Create loop fringe on the bottom starting at the center. Create a loop with a count of 23 teal 11° beads, the bottom sequence, and 23 teal 11° beads. Repeat that same length for the next loop on each side, then reduce the count of teal 11° beads by two for each subsequent loop.

tip

When loop fringe is applied to a curved edge it requires an adjustment to the bead count. In the figures below, loops positioned in the blue area will hang properly (figure 1). However, at some point the curve of the edge lifts one side of the loop. The bottom center of the loop will not hang properly unless you add one or two beads on the upper side of the loop as in figure 2. When you bead along a curved area, change the count of the beads on that side of the loop.

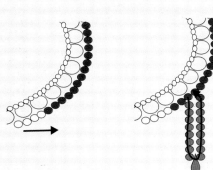

figure 1   figure 2

Lady in
the Forest
Necklace

What You Need

1 aventurine donut round, 36 mm

18 tigereye round beads, 6 mm

16 green and brown jasper flat rectangle beads, 13 x 10 mm

25-inch (63.5 cm) strand of tigereye chip beads, medium size

1 shank-style button, antique bronze, 30 mm

1 piece each of backing and outer-backing, 2¹⁄₄ x 2¹⁄₄ inches (5.7 x 5.7 cm)

Standard Necklace Kit Using Thread (page 15)

Standard Beading Kit (page 14)

Seed Beads

    2 grams of 15° medium gold metallic

    12 grams of 11° green opaque matte

    1 gram of 8° brown transparent

    1 gram of 6° brown transparent

What You Do

1 Glue the donut onto the backing and let it dry.

2 Sew the button in the center of the donut. To stabilize the movement of the button, use the 6° beads between each side of the donut and the shank in a quantity that creates a tight fit. Use doubled thread and stitch up from the back side near the edge of the donut hole. Pick up the fitted 6° beads and button and stitch down on the other side of the hole. Leave the thread loose. Stitch up near the center, through the shank, and down to the back side. Pull on the needle thread and tail thread to tighten it and pull the button into the hole (figure 1). Tie a square knot with the ends, weave in, and cut.

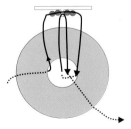

figure 1

3 Create a Standard/Plain Bezel using the 6° beads for the base row and the 15° beads for the bezel row. Stitch an additional row with the 11° beads.

4 Trim the backing. Stabilize if desired. Apply the outer-backing and trim it. Stitch the edge with the 11° beads using the Sunshine Edge stitch. Find and mark the center top and bottom.

5 Create a Turn Bead Attachment using three or four 8° beads at the center top.

6 Create the fringe based on the lesson Stone Fur Fringe below. Use the 11° beads and tigereye chips with a 15° seed for the turn bead. Start in the center bead(s) on the bottom with a core length of 26. Do one more on each side with the same core length, then reduce the subsequent fringes' core count by one. When you get to a core of 22, change to one added branch and alternate the count up using 6, then 10. When you get to a core of 11, use a count-up of 8, not 10. When you get to a core of 8, stop adding branches. When you get to a core of one, use two edge beads.

7 Create the necklace using the Standard Necklace Instructions for Thread (page 144) using the 6-mm, rectangle, and seed beads (figure 2).

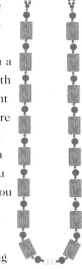

figure 2

Stone Fur Fringe

The basic stitch used here is a Fringe Edge – Branch Fringe Variation, with chips at the end of the fringes and branches. Feel free to substitute other types of beads at the ends for a different look.

1 Start at the center bottom. Add beads until you have the length desired (this is the core); end with a chip (figure 3). Count up six on the core and add a branch using five seeds and a chip. Count up four and add a branch using five seeds and a chip (figure 4). This is a fringe with three chips and is used along the bottom (the red beads in figure 6). Reduce the count for the core as desired.

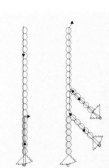

figure 3   figure 4

2 When the edge slopes up the sides of the beadwork (yellow in figure 6), change the fringe to only one branch. Alternate the up count between 6 and 10 (figure 5). Reduce the core count as desired.

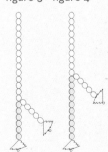

figure 5

3 As you near the edge row because of a reduced core, stop adding branches, shown as the area with the purple beads in figure 6.

figure 6

4 Finally, when you are near the top (the area with the turquoise beads in figure 6), use two edge beads (figure 7).

figure 7

CHAPTER 3

Totem Necklaces

The next stop on the design journey is a design called a totem. This style is characterized by more than one focal lined up on top of each other. Totems are essentially a pendant type of necklace. A simple totem is made of two focals, but it can use many, sort of like a totem pole.

There are three styles of totems. The first, the *drop totem* (photo above, left), is the simplest. It includes two types of focals. One is created with bead embroidery, and the other is attached with a bead strand and drops below.

The second type of totem is a *pieced totem* (photo above, center), and the last is a *consolidated totem* (photo above, right). The difference between these two is the construction method. Each has advantages the other doesn't have, and the selection of which one to use is partly design related and partly personal preference:

• The pieced totem is very bendable and comfortable to wear; there is a natural hinging that happens at the connection areas. A consolidated backing doesn't bend easily and makes for a stiffer pendant. Flexibility is

important when you are creating a long totem because the body is not a flat surface.

• The pieced totem is easier to bead for many people because you are working on smaller components, so it is easier to handle and hold as you are creating the totem elements.

• The consolidated totem has more area between and around the focals, so there is more ability to create different design effects with beads and stitches.

• Piecing a totem is a great method for making last-minute changes. Components can be rearranged into different sequences up until the time they are stitched together. Often focals take on a different proportion or look once they are surrounded by beadwork, and decisions change about which sequence looks best. This is easy to do with a pieced totem.

- A consolidated totem offers more options for bead placement. Focals can be placed close to each other, they can touch, or they can share a base row. In a pieced totem, each focal is beaded as a separate component through to the edge row, so positioning focals close to each other is limited.

- Pieced/component beadwork can be additive. There is an immediate sense of accomplishment as you create the pieces, so it is sort of like candy or potato chips; no one can do just one! If you get tired of making the components, just stop and redesign. If you have extras, use them to make a bracelet or earrings. This will let you use up all those small pieces of backings!

TO DESIGN A TOTEM NECKLACE:

1 Select focals (beads, cabochons, etc.) that you may want to use for your totem. Line them up and arrange them as desired. Try turning the beads horizontally, vertically, or at angles.

2 Assemble other beads you might use. Include beads for the necklace and beads to use on the surface design. Arrange these with the beads chosen in step 1.

3 Select seed beads while keeping in mind the focal and bead color(s) selected in steps 1 and 2. Select the seed bead sizes for the base and bezel rows depending on the profile of the focals.

4 Decide whether you want to create the totem as separate components or with a consolidated backing—or as a combination of the two.

5 Select your techniques for stitches, bezels, edges, and attachments.

6 Review your design plan. You may want to change your selected beads based on the techniques you plan to use.

7 Record your design plan with notes or photos.

Look at the English Garden Necklace on the right on the facing page and photo 1 on page 48. This design began with the rose components. The large rose is so tall that a good design has to consider that aspect. Design is not just about the lines and colors, but also about the changes in the surface heights—the topography. The thick-cut, large bloodstone cabochon satisfied the depth requirement, and the color palette was set.

Assemble the beads you might use.

Seed beads in green and red were added to the pile, and metallic bronze seed beads were selected to provide an accent. Using the same color beads and techniques for the base and bezel rows on each of the stones provides design unity. Fringe at the bottom balances the solid reds above and adds some movement. The bail technique selected is a bold, substantial look that balances the bulk below. In summary, each aspect of design fundamentals from color to balance was considered before the design process was complete.

Arctic Storm Necklace

What You Need

1 porcelain jasper puffed flat oval bead, 40 x 30 mm

1 bone carved Celtic knot link, 32 x 30 mm

1 purple aventurine fan bead, 18 x 20 mm

27 bamboo coral barrel beads, 5 mm

7 bone heishi beads, 4 mm

24 purple aventurine melon-shaped beads, 8 x 10 mm

5 metal rondelles, antique gold, 4 mm

1 piece each of backing and outer-backing, 2½ x 3 inches (6.4 x 7.6 cm)

Standard Necklace Kit with Flexible Beading Wire (page 15)

Standard Beading Kit (page 14)

Seed Beads

 2 grams of 15° medium gold metallic

 2 grams of 11° dark amethyst opaque

 2 grams of 11° amethyst transparent matte

 1 gram of 11° medium gold metallic

 1 gram of 8° dark amethyst opaque

What You Do

1 Glue the porcelain jasper bead onto the backing and let it dry. Sew on with the One-Bead Stitch. Create a Standard/Plain Bezel with the bamboo coral beads for the base row using Couch Stitch and the 15° beads for the bezel row. Add an additional row using the 11° transparent matte beads.

2 Use the Stacks Stitch to add interest to the design. Place the seven stacks between the 3 and 5 o'clock positions (if the center stone were a clock) near the bezel row. (Use figures 1 and 2 as a guide, or arrange them in any area you desire.) The stack consists of one bone heishi bead with an 11° purple opaque for the turn bead.

tip Beads and cabochons are sometimes ground unevenly on the sides. This can be difficult to determine by looking at them, but when surrounded by bead rows, it becomes obvious and looks like a flaw in your workmanship. Adding stacks will hide uneven edges and provide an interesting design to the surface. Buy that damaged focal at a reduced price and use this technique to hide flaws and chips. The best choices for these stacks are heishi beads, rondelles, and disk-shaped beads, because they cover a large area and lie flat.

3 Trim the backing. Apply the outer-backing and trim it. Stitch the edge with the Sunshine Edge stitch using the 11° opaque beads. Find and mark the center top and bottom.

4 Create a Turn Bead Attachment using the 8° beads at the center top. Use figure 3 if the center is between two beads and figure 4 if the center is a bead.

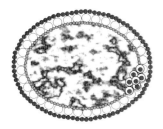

figure 1

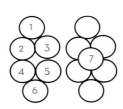

figure 2

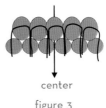

center

figure 3

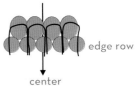

center

figure 4

edge row

5 Attach the Celtic knot at the center bottom using the 11° opaque beads. Stitch from the back side at least ¼ inch (6 mm) from the edge and out the edge bead. Pick up enough beads (six to eight) to position the drop. Stitch through the drop, and pick up enough beads (five to seven) to stitch up to the center. Stitch through the edge bead. Stitch over to the other side of the center using the Running Stitch and repeat, sharing the 11° beads on the back side. Follow figures 5 and 6 if the center is a bead; if the center is between beads, refer to figures 7 and 8. Repeat the thread path to strengthen it. Knot, weave in, and cut the threads.

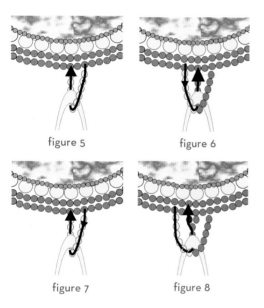

figure 5   figure 6

figure 7   figure 8

6 Stitch through the drop beads (the 4-mm rondelle and the fan bead) and pick up three 15° beads to use as a turn bead. Stitch back up through the drop beads and pick up enough 11° opaque beads to loop around and through the Celtic knot bottom loop. The tail and needle threads are now next to each other (figure 9). Repeat the thread path two more times to strengthen the attachment. Knot the ends, weave in, and cut the thread.

figure 9

7 Finish the edge with the Pointed Edge Stitch using the 11° opaque beads with a 15° at the center top. Start at the bottom near the drop and work to the top. Leave two or three edge beads near the Turn Bead Attachment empty so the necklace strand will not overlap the edge beads.

8 String the necklace using the Standard Necklace Instructions for Flexible Beading Wire (page 145) using the melon-shaped beads, 11° gold seeds, 4-mm rondelles, bamboo coral beads, and 8° opaque seed beads (figure 10).

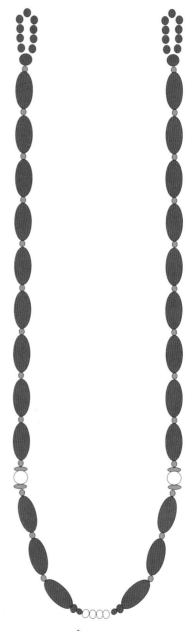

figure 10

Icy Deep Necklace

What You Need

1 cat's-eye glass rounded rectangle cabochon, turquoise, 32 x 21 mm

1 millefiori puffed flat round bead, turquoise and yellow, 10 mm

1 cat's-eye glass square cabochon, turquoise, 14 mm

15 flat leaf beads, center drilled, sea-foam green, 7 x 10 mm

34 freshwater pearl round beads, sea-foam green, 8 mm

22 cat's-eye glass faceted round beads, turquoise, 5 mm

4 metal rondelless, gold, 4 mm

2 glass saturn beads, sea-foam green, 10 mm

1 glass tube bead, light turquoise transparent, 4 x 14 mm

1 piece each of backing and outer-backing, 2½ x 2 inches (6.4 x 5.1 cm)

2 pieces each of backing and outer-backing, 1 x 1 inch (2.5 x 2.5 cm)

Standard Necklace Kit Using Flexible Beading Wire (page 15)

Standard Beading Kit (page 14)

Seed Beads

    7 grams of 15° fancy light green

    3 grams of 11° pale green rainbow

    2 grams of 11° medium gold metallic

    1 gram of 8° medium gold metallic

    1 gram of twisted bugle beads, light turquoise, 12 mm

What You Do

1 Mark center lines horizontally and vertically on the 2½ x 2-inch (6.4 x 5.1 cm) piece of backing. Glue the 32 x 21-mm cabochon in the center and let it dry.

2 The bezel is a combination of the Bead-Across and Bugle Row Bezels. Stitch a base row with the 11° green beads. Stitch a 15° bead at the center sides. Stitch one bugle row using the 15° and bugle beads at the center top and bottom (figure 1). Fill in the bezel row with the 15° beads (figure 2). Stitch two additional rows using the 11° green beads.

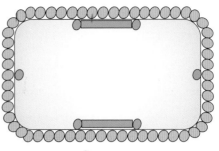

figure 1

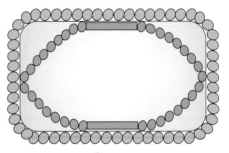

figure 2

> **tip** If the base row is lifting up from the backing, use the Couch Stitch to anchor it down. The Couch Stitch is very valuable to adjust the positioning of any rows of beads previously stitched. Use a tight tension on the thread to pull the row securely into position.

3 Glue the 10-mm millefiori bead in the center of the 1 x 1-inch (2.5 x 2.5 cm) backing and let it dry. Sew the bead on with the One-Bead Stitch. Create a Standard/Plain Bezel with the 8° beads for the base row and the 15° beads for the bezel row. Stitch an additional row with the 15° beads.

4 Glue the square cabochon onto the 1 x 1-inch (2.5 x 2.5 cm) backing and let it dry. Create a Standard/Plain Bezel with the 11° gold beads for the base row and the 15° beads for the bezel row.

5 For each component: Trim the backing. Apply the outer-backing and trim it. Stitch the edge with the Sunshine Edge using the 11° green beads. Find and mark the center tops and bottoms.

6 Stitch a Lace Ruffle Edge on the millefiori component using the 15° beads and a tight tension on the thread so the ruffle holds its shape.

> **tip**
>
> The edge is not an afterthought; it is a key part of the beaded design:
> • Take a variety of focals and use the same seed beads or edge techniques to provide unity in the design.
> • Take focals that are the same and use different edge techniques for design variety.
> • Use heavy, larger techniques (like Rope or Ruffle Edge) to enlarge the design and adjust the proportions.
> • Use edge techniques to add a selected color to the outside for balance.

7 Add a Fringe Edge—Standard Fringe on the bottom of the square cabochon component using the 11° green beads. The end sequence is one 5-mm bead, one 11°, and one leaf bead with the 15° as the turn bead. Start in the center with a count of eighteen 11° beads plus the end sequence. Stitch to the right, reducing the count by two for seven more fringes. Repeat on the left side of the center fringe. Finish the sides with the Pointed Edge; continue for three points, starting next to the fringe. Set this component aside.

> **tip**
>
> Fringe is often heavy, not only because of the weight of the beads, but also because of the centrifugal force pulling out when it moves. To properly secure fringe strands, always stitch into the backings for each strand. Do not just loop over the edge beads. Stitch through the edge bead, staying on the back side. Stitch through the backings straight up at least ¼ inch (6 mm) from the edge to the top side. Stitch over to the next edge bead underneath the surface beading to the next edge bead, through the backings to the back side. Stitch straight down through the edge bead for the next fringe.

8 Create a Square Stitch Bail seven columns wide and 16 beads tall to fit the tube bead. Attach to the center top of the rectangle cabochon with the 5-mm bead inserted between the edge and the bail (figure 3).

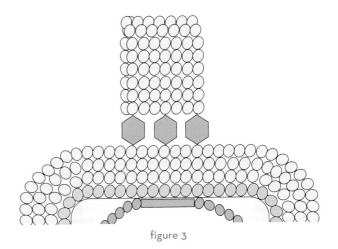

figure 3

9 Use the rectangle cabochon component and Combine at the center bottom to the millefiori bead component's center top. Add seven 11° green beads between the components to provide room for the lace ruffle edge (see photo, below).

10 Combine the center bottom of the millefiori component to the center top of the fringed component. Add six 11° green beads between the components to provide room for the lace ruffle edge (refer to the photo again).

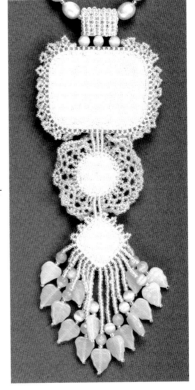

11 Stitch the Circles Edge on the top component. Start two beads after the edge bead used to attach the bail. Continue to the bottom, stopping when the edge overlaps with the lace ruffle.

tip

Choose the sequence of your beading steps to make the beading easier. Consider adding fringes, attachments, and edges before combining. You will be working with smaller pieces that are easier to handle and work with. There are times when these additions need to be done after combining (like step 11) because you need to see the proportions to decide the stopping and starting points.

12 String the necklace using the Standard Necklace Instructions for Flexible Beading Wire (page 145) using the freshwater pearl, 11° green, 11° gold, 4-mm rondelle, saturn, and 5-mm beads as illustrated (figure 4).

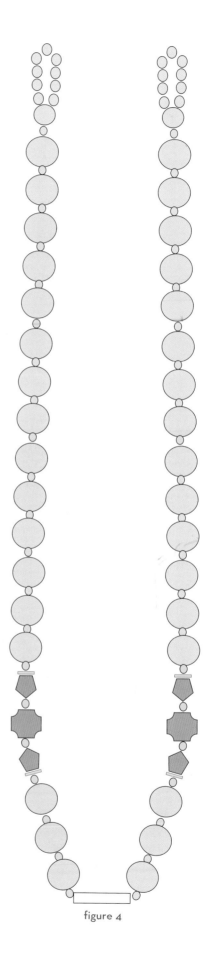

figure 4

44

Swirl'n Necklace

Based on Icy Deep Necklace (page 41)

Key Elements: Rivolis, crystal AB and sapphire, 18 mm; crystal bicone beads, crystal AB, light sapphire, and sapphire, 3 mm

Necklace Strand: Crystal round beads, sapphire, 8 mm; crystal bicone beads, sapphire, 6mm; Standard Necklace Instructions for Flexible Beading Wire (page 145)

Stitches/Techniques: Create a Flat Base Lesson (page 119), Stacks Bezel, Stacks Stitch, Sunshine Edge, Combining, Herringbone Loop Attachment, Side Petal Edge, Rope Edge Size Variation Lesson (below)

Rope Edge Size Variation

Beginning at the edge bead next to the bail, on the left to do a modified rope edge using the 11°, 15°, and 3-mm crystal bicone beads.

1 Start with one 11°, one 15°, one 3-mm, one 15°, and one 11° for the first loop.

2 Increase the count of the 11° beads in the loop by one for the next loop. Repeat that count for the next loop. Continue with this pattern until the middle of the component.

3 At the middle of the component, reduce the count of the 11° beads in the loop by one and repeat that count for the next loop. Continue with that pattern, stitching to one edge bead before the edge combination.

A Rope Edge Size Variation can be done on any size and shape of component. If the component is large, the increase in the loop size may cause the loop to become floppy and not hold the shape. This will work on a bottom component, but it will be a problem on top and middle components. To prevent this, when the increase gets to seven, simply repeat that size loop until you reach the area to decrease the count.

English Garden Necklace

What You Need

1 coral and resin carved rose bead, 25 mm

1 fancy jasper marquis bead, 38 x 16 mm

1 bloodstone cabochon, 10 mm tall in center, 38 x 52 mm

1 dragon's blood jasper teardrop bead, 25 x 19 mm

3 coral carved rose cabochons, 12 mm

11 sponge coral round beads, 5 mm

1 coral leaf bead, top drilled, 23 x 10 mm

1 glass tube bead, green, 15 x 4 mm

36 nephrite jade round beads, 8 mm

1 piece each of backing and outer-backing, 8 x 5 inches (20.3 x 12.7 cm)

Standard Necklace Kit Using Flexible Beading Wire (page 15)

Standard Beading Kit (page 14)

Seed Beads

  2 grams of 15° red luster

  2 grams of 15° bronze metallic

  12 grams of 11° olive transparent

  2 grams of 11° bronze metallic

  4 grams of 8° bronze metallic

  12 grams of 6° bronze metallic

What You Do

The steps in this project include not only the specific steps to make the project, but also the process used to create the design. This will help you to create your own unique totem.

1 Fold a piece of 8½ x 11-inch (21.6 x 27.9 cm) paper in half lengthwise and mark the center line. Unfold the paper and arrange the totem elements on it using the center line as the planned center of the totem. Move the components around until you get a design you like. Plan the stitches and bead sizes around each component to approximate the distances between them and check the arrangement. Decide the final shape. There are two ways to plan the shape used for a consolidated totem. One is to plan the beadwork rows and bead placement, then trim to whatever shape that creates when the beadwork is executed. The other is to decide on a shape, cut to that shape, and fill in beads to meet the shape. This project uses the first method. This doesn't always work exactly as expected, so draw a shape you like on the paper as a backup plan. Refold the paper and cut on the drawn shape for a symmetrical design; otherwise, just cut on the drawn shape for asymmetrical designs. Place the cut shape on the backing and draw around it.

tip Always record your plan. The easiest way is to take a quick photo using your camera or phone; you also can draw out your plan. Include notes for seed bead and stitch selection. These projects are typically not completed in one sitting, and you may need to refer to your plan to refresh your memory.

2 Trace the shape from step 1 onto the backing and draw a center line. Mark some horizontal lines on the backing both as another backup plan and to help bead/focal placement while beading.

tip There are many ways to begin the beading process. One is to glue on all the focals based on the plan. This approach doesn't allow for any adjustments to focal placement, however, or easy changes. Another approach is to glue a focal, execute beading around it, glue on the next focal and bead around it, and repeat until all focals are done. This can be done top to bottom, bottom to top, or most dominant or critical focal first. It is usually best to start with the most dominant, largest, or critical focal and build up and down from there. This project, however, uses a top-to-bottom approach, which also works well.

3 Center the marquis bead 1 inch (2.5 cm) down from the top and glue it down. Let it dry and then sew on with the One-Bead Stitch. The bezel is a combination of the Standard/Plain Bezel and Bead-Across Bezel. Stitch a base row with the 6° gold beads. Manage the spacing on the row, counting the number of beads used on the top, then duplicate that on the bottom. Fill in the corners with 11° bronze beads. Use the 15° red beads to create a partial bezel row on the top and bottom. Finish like a Bead-Across Bezel as illustrated (figure 1).

figure 1

4 Read the lesson Spacing Focals on page 49. Glue down the three coral rose cabochons, positioning them below the previous base row and leaving a space to stitch one row of 11° beads. Create a Standard/Plain Bezel using the 11° olive beads for the base row and the 15° bronze beads for the bezel row (figure 2).

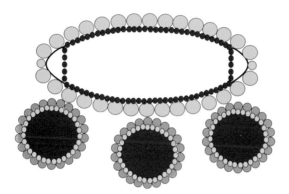

figure 2

5 Glue the bloodstone cabochon below the center coral rose, leaving room for a row of 8° beads. Create a Standard/Plain Bezel using the 8° bronze beads for the base row and the 15° red beads for the bezel row.

6 The big rose-bead petals will sit over the base rows of the focal above and below it. Set the rose on the backing and mark where to place the teardrop focal below, leaving space for the rose bead and a 6° bead base row on the teardrop. Glue the teardrop on and let it dry. Sew it on with the One-Bead Stitch. Create a Standard/Plain Bezel using the 6° bronze beads for the base row and the 15° red beads for the bezel row (photo 1).

photo 1

7 Glue the rose into position, let it dry, and sew it on with the One-Bead Stitch. Stitch a row of Backstitch around the base using the 8° bronze beads. Using the 11° olive beads, stitch an additional row around the bottom teardrop. Stitch two additional rows around the bloodstone cabochon using the 11° olive beads. Stitch an additional row above the top marquis using the 11° olive beads.

8 Review the progress and decide the final shape. Mark cut lines for areas not determined by the beadwork and trim (photos 2, 3, and 4).

photo 2

photo 3

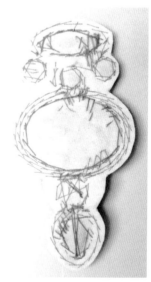

photo 4

9 Fill in the top area around the rose cabochons with Picot Stitch using the 11° olive beads. Fill in the area around the large rose with Backstitch rows using the 11° olive beads, starting at the edge and working toward the center.

10 Apply the outer-backing and trim. Stitch the edge with the Sunshine Edge stitch using the 11° olive beads. Find and mark the center top and bottom.

11 At the center bottom, stitch a Fringe Edge—Loop Fringe using three 11° olive, one 11° bronze, one coral leaf, one 11° bronze, and three 11° olive beads over a base of two or three center edge beads. Add a Fringe Edge—Standard Fringe on both sides. Start with a bead count of nine 11° beads and an end sequence of one 11° bronze bead, one 5-mm coral bead, and an 11° bronze turn bead. Reduce the count by two for subsequent fringes. Complete four fringes on each side.

12 Create a Square Stitch Bail seven columns wide and 16 beads tall to cover the tube bead. Attach to the center top with 5-mm coral beads in between (photo 5).

13 Finish the edge with the Pointed Edge Stitch using the 11° olive beads with a 15° bronze bead for the center top.

14 String the necklace following the Standard Necklace Instructions for Flexible Beading Wire (page 145), using the 8-mm round, 11° bronze, and tube beads (figure 3).

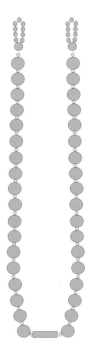

figure 3

photo 5

lesson

Spacing Focals

It's not difficult to manage the placement of focals. If a row of beads will be positioned around a focal, put a temporary strand of those beads in place to provide accurate spacing. Use paper to create a template for the focal. Position the template as desired, matching the center lines and using the horizontal lines to make sure the focal is level. Trace the outline, then glue the focal inside the traced area.

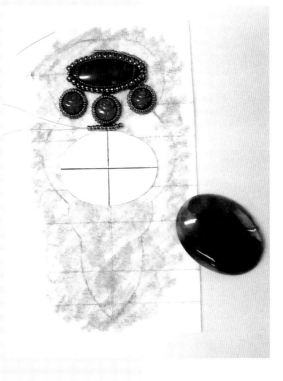

CHAPTER 4

The Many Necklaces

One of the best things about bead embroidery is the opportunity to use many types of beads and focals in one beautiful piece. Numerous stitch techniques add to the range of looks you can achieve with your creations. In this and the next two chapters we will explore the vast variety of "the many."

Designing for "the many" can be challenging only because there are so many starting points and so many possible results. Your starting point might be a desire to use certain beads and focals, or you might want to do a certain shape, bib, or collar. The starting point or source of inspiration can be everywhere and everything. This may sound chaotic, but organize using the steps below and you'll feel confident in the process. Complete each step—but do the steps in any order that makes sense for your starting inspiration.

The design steps for necklaces with many focals include the following:

1 Select focals (beads, cabochons, etc.) that you may want to use.

2 Assemble other beads you might use. Include beads for the necklace section (if applicable) and beads to use on the surface design.

3 Select seed beads, keeping in mind the bead color (or colors) selected above. Select the seed bead sizes for the base and bezel rows depending on the profile of the focals.

4 Decide on a basic shape or format, such as a collar or bib. Decide whether you want to create by combining separate components, by using a consolidated backing, or by using a combination of the two.

5 Arrange the beads, focals, and other elements to plan their placement.

6 Select techniques for stitches, bezels, edges, and attachments.

7 Review your design plan and make patterns using paper. Try on the pattern where applicable. Change the selected beads as necessary based on the planned techniques.

8 Record your design plan with notes or photos.

tip

For a valuable size perspective, use the Neck Circle or Neck Form Page (see page 12) to help design multifocal necklaces. If you are considering doing a collar, mark the inside circle of a Collar Form (see page 13) on the Neck Form Page.

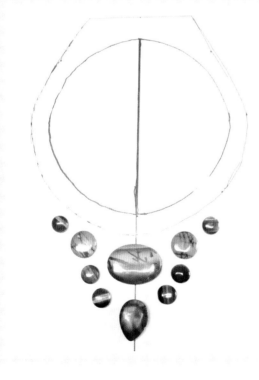

Panel Collar Necklace

What You Need

1 red agate Quan Yin carved pendant, 40 x 28 mm

1 red agate carved lead pendant, 25 x 34 mm

1 sodalite puffed flat marquis bead, 40 x 20 mm

2 sodalite puffed flat rectangle beads, 25 x 28 mm

2 sodalite puffed flat oval beads, 12 x 16 mm

2 red agate puffed flat teardrop beads, top or center drilled, 28 x 30 mm

4 red agate cabochons, 13 x 18 mm

27 red agate faceted beads, 6 mm

20 red agate faceted beads, 8 mm

2 sodalite round beads, 6 mm

2 metal rondelles, light gold, 6 mm

8 metal ribbed bead caps, 6 mm

1 piece each of backing and outer-backing, 4 x 3 inches (10.2 x 7.6 cm)

2 pieces each of backing and outer-backing, 3 x 2½ inches (7.6 x 6.4 cm)

2 pieces each of backing and outer-backing, 2½ x 2 inches (6.4 x 5.1 cm)

2 pieces each of backing and outer-backing, 2 x 2 inches (5.1 x 5.1 cm)

Standard Necklace Kit Using Thread (page 15)

Standard Beading Kit (page 14)

Seed Beads

    3 grams of 15° light gold metallic

    1 gram of 15° cobalt luster

    9 grams of 11° light gold metallic

    30 grams of 11° cobalt luster

    10 grams of 6° dark blue opaque matte

What You Do

1 Create patterns for the panels using paper. Use the chart below, and mark the measurements on the fold of the paper. Connect the markings as illustrated by the red lines (figure 1). Cut on the lines while the paper is folded. Use the unfolded pattern to trace the appropriate quantity (indicated in the chart) onto the backing. Cut the backing as traced and mark the vertical centers.

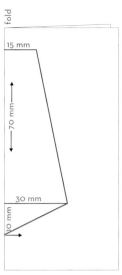

figure 1

top line length from fold	length down fold	bottom line length from fold	length down fold	quantity
15 mm	70 mm	30 mm	10 mm	1
15 mm	60 mm	25 mm	5 mm	2
12 mm	50 mm	20 mm	5 mm	2
12 mm	40 mm	18 mm	5 mm	2
10 mm	30 mm	15 mm	5 mm	2

2 Stitch a row of Backstitch on the edge of each panel using the 11° gold beads.

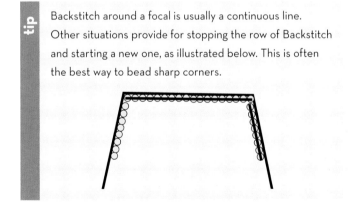

tip

Backstitch around a focal is usually a continuous line. Other situations provide for stopping the row of Backstitch and starting a new one, as illustrated below. This is often the best way to bead sharp corners.

MAKE THE CENTER PANEL (MAKE 1)

3 Center and glue the Quan Yin pendant below the edge row, leaving room for two rows of Backstitch using the 11° beads. Let it dry. Create a Standard/Plain Bezel using the 11° cobalt beads for the base row and 15° gold beads for the bezel row.

4 Center and glue the marquis bead below the Quan Yin pendant, leaving room for one row of 6° beads. Let it dry and stitch it on with the One-Bead Stitch. Create a Standard/Plain Bezel using the 6° beads for the base row and the 15° gold beads for the bezel row. Center three 6-mm faceted beads below the marquis and sew on using the One-Bead Stitch. Stitch an additional row using the 11° cobalt beads.

5 Stitch additional rows of Backstitch using the 11° cobalt beads to fill in as illustrated (figure 2). Use the bead caps cup-side up and an 11° gold for the turn bead with the Stacks Stitch, and add two stacks on each side of the 6-mm faceted beads below the marquis.

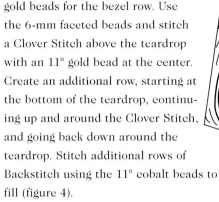

figure 2

MAKE THE LARGEST SIDE PANELS (MAKE 2)

6 Glue the red agate cabochon at the center bottom, leaving room for one row of 11° beads. Let it dry. Create a Standard/Plain Bezel using the 11° cobalt beads for the base row and the 15° gold beads for the bezel row.

7 Center and glue the sodalite rectangle above the cabochon, leaving room for one row of 6° beads. Let it dry and stitch it on with the One-Bead Stitch. Create a Standard/Plain Bezel using the 6° beads for the base row and the 15° gold beads for the bezel row. Use the 6-mm faceted beads and stitch a Clover Stitch above the rectangle with an 11° gold bead at the center.

8 Stitch additional rows of Backstitch using the 11° cobalt beads to fill as illustrated (figure 3). Use the bead caps cup-side up and an 11° gold for the turn bead with the Stacks Stitch, and add a stack on each side of the cabochon.

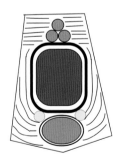

figure 3

MAKE THE NEXT LARGEST PANELS (MAKE 2)

9 Glue the teardrop onto the center bottom, leaving room for one row of 6° beads. Let it dry and sew on with the One-Bead Stitch. Create a Standard/Plain Bezel using the 6° beads for the base row and the 15°

gold beads for the bezel row. Use the 6-mm faceted beads and stitch a Clover Stitch above the teardrop with an 11° gold bead at the center. Create an additional row, starting at the bottom of the teardrop, continuing up and around the Clover Stitch, and going back down around the teardrop. Stitch additional rows of Backstitch using the 11° cobalt beads to fill (figure 4).

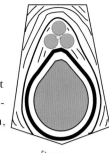

figure 4

MAKE THE SIDE-BACK PANELS (MAKE 2)

10 Glue the sodalite oval on the center bottom, leaving room for one row of 6° beads. Let it dry and sew it on with the One-Bead Stitch. Create a Standard/Plain Bezel using the 6° beads for the base row and the 15° gold beads for

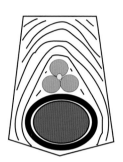

figure 5

the bezel row. Use the 6-mm faceted beads and stitch a Clover Stitch above the oval with an 11° gold bead at the center. Create an additional row, starting at the bottom of the oval, continuing up and around the Clover Stitch, and going back down around the oval. Stitch additional rows of Backstitch using the 11° cobalt beads to fill (figure 5).

> **tip**
>
> When filling an area, complete the rows first. Go back later and stitch extra beads with the One-Bead Stitch into the blank areas. Use thick or thin beads to fit and turn them in any way needed to fill the space. Use smaller beads (typically 15°) of the same color to fit in tiny areas.

MAKE THE FINAL, SMALLEST SECTIONS (MAKE 2)

11 Glue a red agate cabochon on the center bottom, leaving room for one row of 11° beads. Let it dry. Create a Standard/ Plain Bezel using the 11° cobalt beads for the base row and the 15° gold beads for the bezel row. Use the 6-mm faceted beads and stitch a Clover Stitch above the oval with an 11° gold bead at the center. Create an additional row around the cabochon. Stitch additional rows of Backstitch using the 11° cobalt beads to fill (figure 6).

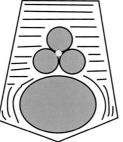

figure 6

12 For each panel: Apply the outer-backing and trim it. Stitch the edge with the Sunshine Edge stitch using 11° cobalt beads.

13 Arrange the panels around your Neck Circle (page 12) to test the fit (photo 1).

photo 1

14 The standard design Combines the panels using one 8-mm bead in between each panel, with another strand (an 8-mm expanded with an 11° cobalt on each side) positioned three beads underneath. The closure consists of a Herringbone Loop Attachment—Sideways Loop Variation that is 12 beads tall above an 8-mm bead (figure 7). The closure includes a hook and an adjustable 4-inch (10.2 cm) chain.

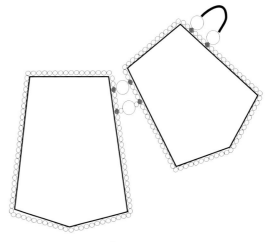

figure 7

Other options to adjust the fit include using a 6-mm instead of an 8-mm bead, eliminating the bead on the loop closure, adding extra beads to Combine, or adding a longer extension chain in back. Adjust as needed.

15 Use jump rings to attach the hook and chain to the end loops.

> **tip** This project can be done by eliminating some of the panels for many other design possibilities.

project Variation

Serpent Necklace

Based on Panel Collar Necklace (page 52)

Key Elements: Lampwork glass snake pendant, green, 66 x 35 mm; cloisonné leaf beads, green, 27 x 16 mm; glass round beads for fringe drops, light green AB, 3 mm, 4 mm, and 6 mm; glass teardrop bead for fringe drop, light green AB, 11 x 8 mm

Necklace Strand: Glass round beads, green AB, 8 mm; Standard Necklace Instructions for Direct Attachment Sunshine Edge—Two Edge Beads (page 146)

Stitches/Techniques: Backstitch, Picot Stitch, Sunshine Edge, Fringe Edge, surface stitching based on Whimsical Collar Necklace (page 80)

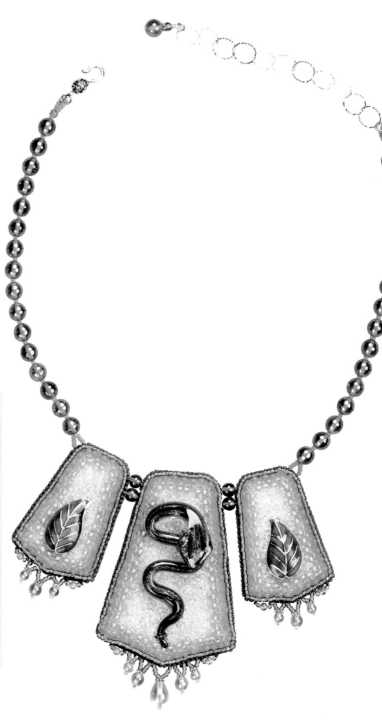

lesson

Filling with Picot Stitch

To fill an area using the Picot Stitch, stitch around the border, changing the direction of the stitch. Then fill the center, changing direction and angle as needed (figures 1 and 2).

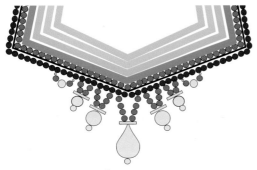

figure 1   figure 2

Use the diagrams below to finish the bottom edges. Use figure 3 for the center panel, and figure 4 for the side panels.

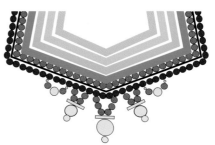

figure 3   figure 4

Leaf
Cascade
Necklace

What You Need

1 moukaite carved rose bead, 19 mm

150 to 170 olive new jade round beads, 4 mm

36 freshwater pearl beads, 8 mm

30 to 35 mother-of-pearl leaf beads, top and side drilled, 30 x 15 mm

1 glass tube bead, crystal or beige, 22 x 5 mm

1 piece each of backing and outer-backing, 6 x 3 inches (15.2 x 7.6 cm)

Standard Necklace Kit Using Flexible Beading Wire (page 15)

Standard Beading Kit (page 14)

Seed Beads

  1 gram of 15° opaque luster cream

  35 grams of 11° opaque luster cream

  5 grams of 11° dusty rose color-lined

  5 grams of 11° gold/olive color-lined

  2 grams of 8° dusty rose opaque

What You Do

1 Create a pattern using paper folded in half. Mark the measurements shown in figure 1 (½ inch=1.3cm, 5¾ inch=14.6cm, 1¼ inches=3.2cm), and connect the markings as illustrated by the red line. Cut on the outline while folded. Unfold and trace the shape onto the backing. Cut out the backing as traced and mark the vertical center.

2 Center the rose ¼ inch (6 mm) from the top, glue it down, and let it dry. Sew it on with the One-Bead Stitch. Use the 4-mm beads and create a row around it using the Couch Stitch. Use the 11° cream beads and stitch an additional row of Backstitch around the Couch Stitch row.

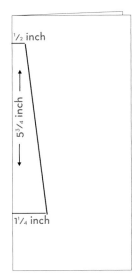

figure 1

tip Rows of round beads create gaps where the backing can show through. Using an 11° or a 15° bead in a coordinating color, stitch a bead in between the round beads to cover that area. Do this after you have stitched the surrounding row to completely define the area you need to cover. Use the 15° cream beads and the One-Bead Stitch to fill the gaps as illustrated in red in figure 2, above. This is optional, but it will create a more finished, professional appearance.

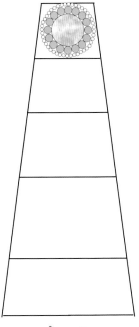

figure 2

3 Draw a horizontal line just under the additional row of cream seed beads. Draw another line 1 inch (2.5 cm) below that. Draw another line 1¼ inches (3.2 cm) below that, and a fourth line 1½ inches (3.8 cm) below that (figure 3).

figure 3

tip Be careful when putting marks on backings if you are using light-colored backings and beads. Use light-colored pens so the lines don't show through the beadwork. If you don't have a pen that is light enough, use the Running Stitch with white thread to mark the lines. You'll be able to see the thread line, but it won't show after the beading is complete. This also works for marking lines on black backing, using black thread.

4 Read the lesson Fringe Setup Row, page 61. Use the 11° cream beads and stitch a fringe setup row on each drawn line. Stitch across the entire line.

5 Fill the rest of the surface with the 11° cream beads. Use the Backstitch and stitch curves around the top. For the spaces below, use a five-bead Lazy Stitch. Stitch the edges first starting at the bottom and working upward (figures 4 and 5). Adjust the bead count on the stitch to fill the center. See the Tip below for more information.

> **tip**
>
> When filling a space, evaluate the area and make decisions that make your beading easier. This area will be mostly hidden under the fringe, so speed versus appearance is more important, and a fast stitch—like the Lazy Stitch—is perfect. To get a good fit, start at the bottom of the area. If there are any issues regarding fit, they will be positioned under the fringe setup row, which will be covered by fringe. If there is a small space that won't fit an 11° bead, use 15° beads in the last row. Similarly, start at the edges, then work toward the center. Put the fit issues in an area that is easy to evaluate and bead.

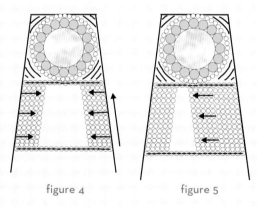

figure 4   figure 5

6 Use doubled thread to add the loop fringe. The fringe consists of the 11°, 4-mm round, and leaf beads. There are two designs for the loop bottom, used every other one. One design is three rose, one olive, one 4 mm, two olive, one 4 mm (the middle), two olive, one 4 mm, one olive, and three rose (figure 6). The other is the same but replaces the 4 mm in the middle with the leaf (figure 7). Start at the right on the top row. The first fringe is a count of two cream, the loop bottom with leaf, and a count of two cream. The count does not

include the fringe setup bead, so a count of two will result in a fringe that is three cream. The next fringes increase the count of the cream on each side of the loop by one. Alternate the bottom middle with the 4 mm, then leaf, then 4 mm, leaf, and so on. Start at the second bead in on the fringe setup row and stitch as illustrated in figure 8 to provide for a secure base for the fringe.

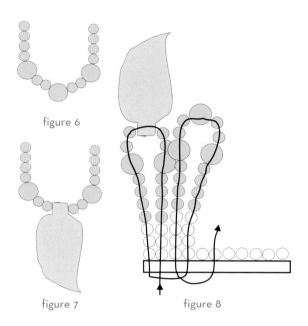

figure 6

figure 7   figure 8

> **tip**
>
> If there is an odd number of beads in the fringe setup row, share a bead on one of the loops as illustrated in figure 9. Do this adjustment in an area that is least obvious. For this project the least obvious is the third loop in from the end of the row. As a general rule, adjustments are obvious on the first and last loops. They are also more obvious on short loops than on long ones.

figure 9

7 Repeat step 6 on the next fringe setup row except start from the left. Begin with a count of five cream beads and increase by one for the next fringes.

8 Repeat step 6 on the third fringe setup row. Begin from the right with a count of seven and increase by one for the next fringes.

9 Repeat step 6 on the last setup row except start from the left. Begin with a count of 10 cream beads and increase by two for the next fringes.

10 Apply the outer-backing and trim. Edge with the 11° cream beads using the Sunshine Edge on the top and bottom and the Clean Edge stitch on the sides.

11 Repeat step 6 on the bottom edge for the final row of fringe. Start at the right with a count of 20 cream beads and increase by two for the next fringes. Include the beads on each side that were added by the Clean Edge in step 10 as an edge bead to stitch fringe into.

12 Create a Square Stitch Bail with the 11° cream beads that is 16 beads tall. Count the number of edge beads on the top edge and use that for your column count. Attach to the edge with the 4-mm beads in between. Use one each on the first and last columns. Add at least two more. The illustrations show spacing for 12 columns (figure 10) and 13 columns (figure 11).

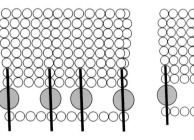

figure 10   figure 11

13 String the necklace using the Standard Necklace Instructions for Flexible Beading Wire (page 145) using 18 pearls alternating with 11° olive beads on each side of the necklace. Use the tube bead in the middle and string though the bail.

Fringe Setup Row

Fringe within the surface of beadwork can be stunning, but trying to do other beading while avoiding fringe strands can be a nightmare: they get in the way and grab the thread. To manage this, create a fringe setup row. This will determine how many fringes to do and reserve the space for the fringe. Do all other beadwork and add the fringe strands as the last step in the surface beadwork.

1 Draw a line on the backing where you want the fringe setup row to be.

2 Stitch up from the back side two beads from the end of the line. Pick up two beads and stitch down near the end of the line as shown in figure 12.

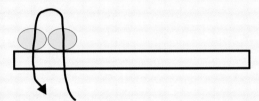

figure 12

3 Stitch up from the back side on the line, leaving space for one bead. Pick up one bead and stitch down through the previous bead as shown in figure 13.

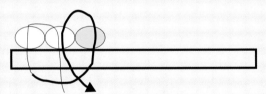

figure 13

4 Repeat step 3 across the line.

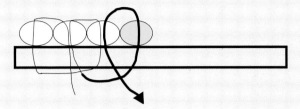

figure 14

The setup row applies the beads onto the surface with the hole side up, as shown in figure 15. The first and last beads in the row have a tendency to roll up. Simply push them back down to maintain the spacing. Once the fringe is stitched on, this won't be an issue.

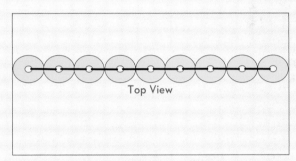

figure 15

My Fair
Lady
Necklace

What You Need

1 genuine shell carved cameo, 24 x 30 mm

1 red agate carved flower, center drilled, 35 x 50 mm

1 red jasper oval cabochon, 12 x 16 mm

2 red aventurine round cabochons, 20 mm

3 red aventurine carved fan beads, 20 x 18 mm

2 red aventurine oval beads, 6 x 8 mm

10 riverstone heishi-cut beads, 4 x 2 mm

27 red aventurine round beads, 4 mm

15 red aventurine round beads, 6 mm

18 red aventurine round beads, 8 mm

1 piece each of backing and outer-backing, 3 x 5 inches (7.6 x 12.7 cm)

2 pieces each of backing and outer-backing, 2 x 2½ inches (5.1 x 6.4 cm)

2 pieces each of backing and outer-backing, 1½ x 1½ inches (3.8 x 3.8 cm)

Standard Necklace Kit Using Thread (page 15)

Standard Beading Kit (page 14)

Seed Beads

  3 grams of 15° gold luster copper

  1 gram of 15° gold color-lined rust luster

  25 grams of 11° gold color-lined rust luster

  2 grams of 11° rust opaque

  2 grams of 8° rust opaque

  6 grams of 6° rust opaque

What You Do

1 Read the lesson Victorian Drape Designs (page 67) to understand the process and terminology.

CREATE THE CENTER (1 EACH)

2 Take the largest backing and mark a vertical center line. Position the cameo in the center, 1 inch (2.5 cm) above the bottom edge. Glue it down and let it dry. Create a Standard/Plain Bezel using the 8° or 6° beads as needed for the base row. Use the 15° copper beads for the bezel row. Stitch an additional row using the 11° luster beads.

tip Many times focals like this cameo (also ammonites, shells, tumbled stones, etc.) have an uneven height on the edge. Use different sizes of beads in the base row to result in a proper elevation of the bezel row.

3 Position the flower above the cameo, centered and touching the additional row. Glue it down and let it dry. Create a Standard/Plain Bezel using the 11° luster beads for the base row and the 15° beads for the bezel row. Use the Stacks Stitch in the center drill with one 6° and a 15° for the turn bead. Because the center stack will help hold the focal to the surface, the bezel row does not need to extend over the entire edge of the flower.

4 Position the red jasper cabochon above the flower, centered and leaving room for a row of 6° beads. Create a Standard/Plain Bezel using the 6° beads for the base row and the 15° beads for the bezel row. Stitch an additional row using the 11° luster beads.

5 Use the Stacks Stitch with the heishi beads and the 15° copper for the turn bead. Add three stacks as shown in figure 1.

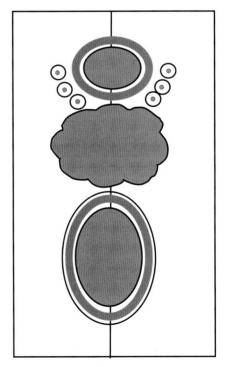

figure 1

6 Draw the final shape. Use the beading under the cameo to determine the bottom edge, and draw above it, leaving room for one row on top (figure 2). Trim on the line.

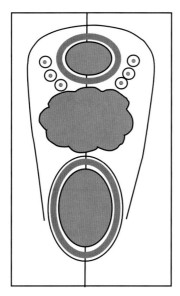

figure 2

> **tip**
>
> Some people can easily draw shapes and make them symmetrical. For those of us who can't, there is a process to help: Place a piece of paper over the beadwork. Draw the shape on it as best as you can using a marker. Hold the paper up to the light and fold it in half, matching the lines drawn as much as possible. Cut the paper while folded. Use the outer border of the paper and place it over your beadwork like a window. If it doesn't work, get a new piece of paper, using the previous paper to help judge the adjustments you need to make. Once you get the frame you want, trace the outline of the paper onto the backing.

7 Use the 11° luster beads and stitch a row of Backstitch around the top outer edge. Fill the remaining area with Picot Stitch using the 11° luster beads (figure 3).

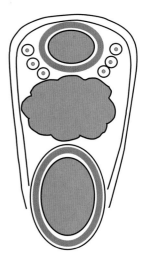

figure 3

CREATE THE SIDE COMPONENTS (2 EACH)

8 Take the next largest backing and mark a vertical center line. Position the fan bead in the center, ½ inch (1.3 cm) from the top. Glue it down and let it dry. Sew on with the One-Bead Stitch. Create a Standard/Plain Bezel using the 6° beads for the base row and the 15° beads for the bezel row. Stitch an additional row using the 11° luster beads.

9 Position the 6 x 8-mm oval in the center, beneath the fan bead and leaving room for a row of 11° beads. Glue it down and let it dry. Sew on with the One-Bead Stitch. Create a Standard/Plain Bezel using the 11° luster beads for the base row and the 15° beads for the bezel row. Use the Stacks Stitch with the heishi beads and the 15° copper for the turn bead. Add two stacks (figure 4).

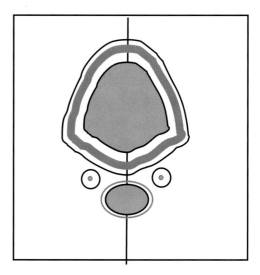

figure 4

10 Stitch a row of Backstitch using the 11° luster beads around the beadwork. Fill the remaining area with Picot Stitch using the 11° luster beads. Trim around the row to the final shape (figure 5).

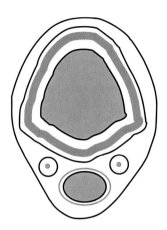

figure 5

CREATE THE END COMPONENTS (2 EACH)

11 Glue the 20-mm cabochon onto the backing and let it dry. Create a Standard/Plain Bezel using the 11° luster beads for the base row and the 15° beads for the bezel row. Trim the backing.

ASSEMBLE THE COMPONENTS

12 For each of the components: Apply the outer-backing and trim it. Use the 11° luster beads and stitch a Sunshine Edge row. Find and mark the center top and bottom.

13 Use your Neck Form Page (see page 12) and arrange the components around it. The connection strand is one 11° luster, one 4 mm, one 6 mm, one 4 mm, and one 11° luster.

• Connect the center to the side component: Count 10 edge beads from the center top of the center component. Stitch through the eleventh edge bead and pick up the connection strand beads. Stitch over to the side component. Count 12 beads from the center top of the side component. Stitch through the thirteenth bead.

• Connect the side component to the end component: Count three edge beads from the center top of the side component. Stitch through the fourth edge bead and pick up the connection strand beads. Stitch over to the end component. Count three edge beads from the center top of the end component and stitch through the fourth edge bead.

• Add the necklace strand: Use nine 8-mm beads alternated with 11° luster beads for the bead strand. Use the Standard Necklace Instructions for Direct Attachment Sunshine Edge—Two Edge Beads (page 146). Use the fourth and sixth edge beads, counted from the center top. Use jump rings and attach the hook and chain.

14 Try on the necklace or put it on a neck form.

tip Instead of tying off and ending threads, wrap the thread around sticky notes so they are available for use later.

15 Use the red aventurine and 11° luster beads to create the drapes. Use the chart below and the edge beads designated in red in figure 6.

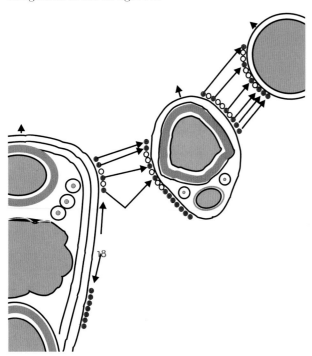

figure 6

Drapes from the center component to the side component

Stress connection (already done): one 11°, one 4 mm, one 6 mm, one 4 mm, one 11°

Top drape: one 11°, one 4 mm, one 6 mm, one 4 mm, two 11°

Next drape: two 11°, one 4 mm, one 6 mm, one 4 mm, three 11°

Next drape (this drape is stitched differently): Pick up seven 11°, one 4 mm, one 6 mm, and one 11°. Stitch back through the 6 mm and 4 mm using the final 11° as a turn bead. Pick up fourteen 11°.

Next drape: forty-two 11°

Next drape: forty-five 11°

Next drape: forty-eight 11°

Next drape: fifty-two 11°

Next drape: fifty-seven 11°

Next drape: sixty-two 11°

Last drape: sixty-seven 11°

Drapes from the side component to the end component

Stress connection (already done): one 11°, one 4 mm, one 6 mm, one 4 mm, one 11°

Top drape: one 11°, one 4 mm, one 6 mm, one 4 mm, one 11°

Next drape: two 11°, one 4 mm, one 6 mm, one 4 mm, two 11°

Next drape: seventeen 11°

Next drape: twenty 11°

Next drape: twenty-three 11°

16 Add the drop to the center bottom of the center component using the 11° luster beads and the fan bead as illustrated (figure 7).

figure 7

Victorian Drape Designs

The critical step in the design of a Victorian drape-style necklace involves combining the components at the stress connections, which includes the back necklace strands. Stress connections are the part of the design that hold the shape and determine the size of the necklace and the orientation of the hanging components. They are designated by the bold lines in figures 8 through 11. Notice in particular how the components hang differently in figures 8 and 9 by changing where the stress connection is attached.

First create your components—three or more—and arrange them using the Neck Form Page (page 12). For each component, identify the spot that will connect that component with the next with a straight line. That is the stress connection. Because these are the connections that will hold all of the weight of the necklace, repeat the thread paths at least four times when using single thread. Complete all of the stress connections first and then attach the back necklace strand. Try the necklace on. Make sure the fit is correct and the components hang with the desired orientation. Make any adjustments needed before proceeding.

The next step is to add the drapes. The easiest method is to put the necklace on a display neck like the one in the photo on page 65. This will help you judge the design, determine how many beads to use in the drape, and select the edge beads to use for each drape. You can use a flat surface (the Neck Form Page), but be aware that the distance you are traveling on the flat surface is farther than it will be when worn, because the body is more of a cone shape, not a flat table. This results in a deeper drape when it is put on an actual neck rather than on the flat surface. Compensate for that when designing your drapes if using the flat Neck Form Page. It is a good idea to try on the necklace periodically as you are creating to make sure you are achieving the desired look. This is helpful no matter which method you select.

Use single thread to stitch all the drapes. Start with the top drape and work down to the bottom drape. Test by trying on the necklace, and make any desired adjustments. When you have the desired drapes, repeat the thread path one or two more times to reinforce and strengthen it. Use your judgment on how many times to repeat based on the weight and length of the drapes (more weight and/or length equals more repeats).

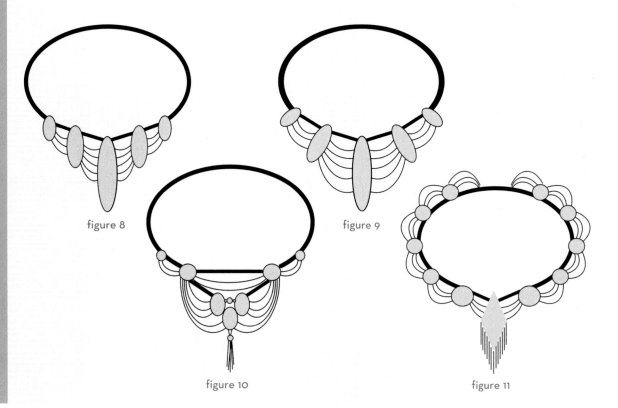

figure 8

figure 9

figure 10

figure 11

CHAPTER 5

Bead Collection Necklaces

Bead collections—either you already have one or you will someday.
Collections can consist of anything from a shape (like leaves or fruit), a color
or colors (like black and white), a particular stone, a glass artist, a passion
(like fishing), or whatever strikes your fancy.

As time goes by, beads are added to the collection. It may take months or even years, but a time will come when the collection reaches critical mass and it's time to create something with those beads.

The easiest collection to identify is a strand or strands of beads. Often purchasing a strand of beads in a puffed flat oval or round is not much more than the cost of just one cabochon of the same stone. A collection of strands of red creek jasper is pictured, right. Beads from those strands were used in the Magic Forest Necklace (page 69) and the Indian Summer Necklace (page 78).

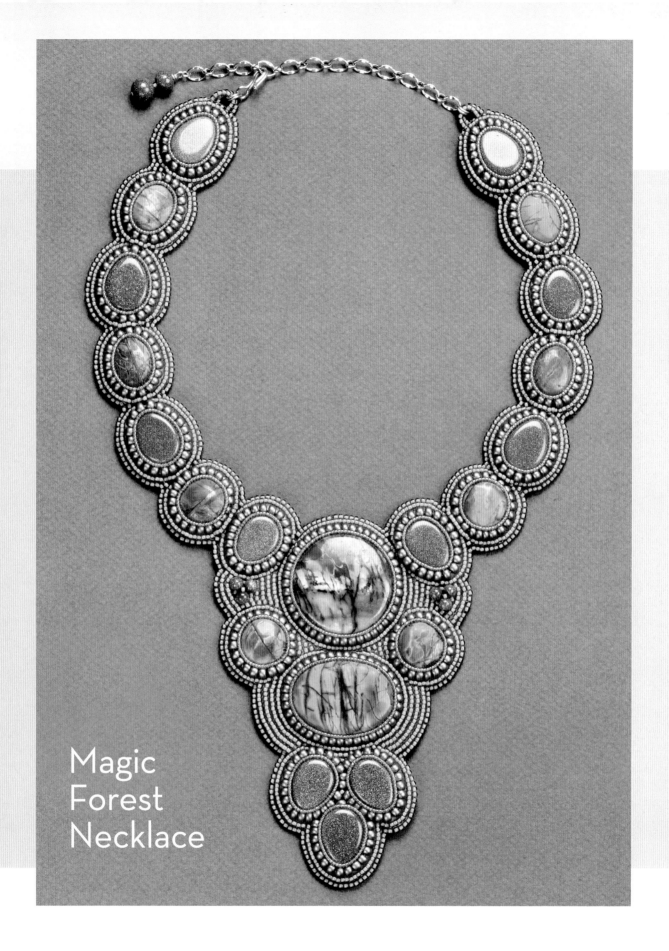

Magic
Forest
Necklace

What You Need

1 red creek jasper puffed flat round bead, 35 mm

1 red creek jasper puffed flat oval bead, 25 x 35 mm

4 red creek jasper puffed flat round beads, 16 mm

4 red creek jasper puffed flat oval beads, 12 x 18 mm

11 goldstone puffed flat teardrop beads, 14 x 18 mm

6 goldstone round beads, 4 mm

1 piece each of backing and outer-backing, 8½ x 13 inches (21.6 x 33 cm)

Standard Necklace Kit Using Thread (page 15)

Standard Beading Kit (page 14)

Seed Beads

    5 grams of 15° gold transparent

    20 grams of 11° dark gold color-lined

    30 grams of 6° pale copper metallic matte

What You Do

1 Create a Collar Form as described on page 13 through step 3. Arrange the beads around the collar and record the arrangement with notes or a photo. The plan is to bead around the stones, and trim based on that profile. Draw a collar shape around the focals for a backup plan. Make it wide enough in the front to add rows or other stitches and in the back collar section make it at least 1½ inches (3.8 cm) wide. Fold the paper on the center line and cut it out so both sides are the same (photo 1). This is the pattern for the collar.

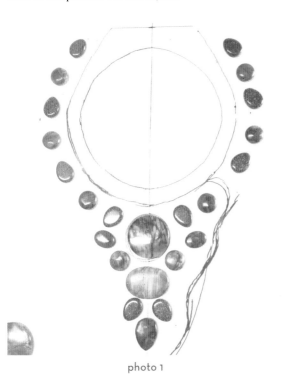

photo 1

 tip Buy rolls of gift wrap paper when it goes on sale, making sure the other side is plain white. This is excellent to use when you want a large surface of inexpensive white paper.

2 Place the pattern on the backing, trace it, and cut it out. If the size of your backing is smaller than your pattern, read the lesson Joining Pieces of Backing (page 73). Mark the vertical center line on the backing plus several horizontal lines.

3 Center the 35-mm round ½ inch (1.3 cm) below the top edge of the backing.

4 Glue the bead on and let it dry. Sew it on with the One-Bead Stitch. Create a Standard/Plain Bezel using the 6° beads for the base row and the 15° beads for the bezel row. Stitch an additional row using the 11° beads.

5 Center the oval below the 35-mm round, leaving room for a row of 6° beads, and repeat step 4.

6 Position the 16-mm rounds on each side, leaving room for a row of 6° beads, and repeat step 4 (figure 1).

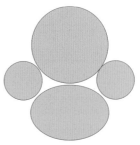

figure 1

7 Position the teardrop beads below the oval (figure 2), leaving room for a 6° row.

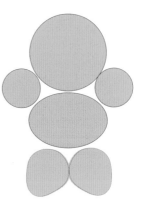

figure 2

8 Position another teardrop bead below the two just added, leaving room for a 6° row (figure 3). Glue them down and let them dry. Sew them on with the One-Bead Stitch. Create a Standard/Plain Bezel using the 6° beads for the base row and 15° beads for the bezel row. Stitch an additional row around below the group of three teardrops using the 11° beads.

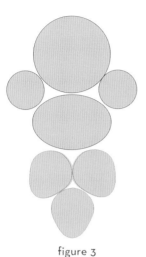

figure 3

9 Position the teardrop beads next to the 35-mm round as illustrated in figure 4, ½ inch (1.3 cm) from the neck edge and leaving room for a row of 6° beads between the teardrop and the existing beadwork. Repeat step 4.

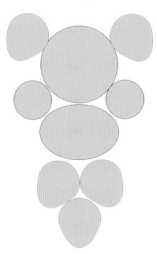

figure 4

10 Complete adding the focals one at a time around the back of the neck in the following order: start with the 16-mm round, then the teardrop, the oval, the teardrop, the oval, and finally a teardrop (figure 5). Position the beads ½ inch (1.3 cm) down from the neck edge, leaving room for a row of 6° beads between the new

focal and the existing beadwork. For each focal: Glue the bead on and let it dry. Sew on with the One-Bead Stitch. Create a Standard/Plain Bezel using the 6° beads for the base row and 15° beads for the bezel row. Stitch an additional row using the 11° beads. Do the next focal in the list with the same process and repeat until all of the focals are used.

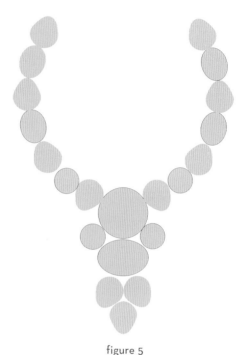

figure 5

11 Stitch two more rows of Backstitch around the bottom oval using the 11° beads. Draw a line on each side from the bottom of the teardrop to the round focal as illustrated in figure 6. Stitch two rows of Backstitch on that edge using the 11° beads. Use the 4-mm round beads with the Clover Stitch and stitch near the two rows just created.

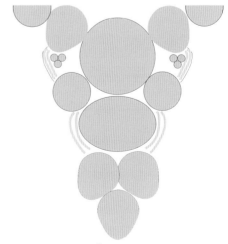

figure 6

When stitching a Backstitch row that needs to butt up against an area already covered, follow these steps to get a tight fit:

- Begin the row approximately one and a half beads away, pick up two beads, and stitch down, leaving room for the beads to slide (figure 7).

figure 7

- Stitch back and up next to the covered area. Pick up two beads and stitch through the two beads already there. Push all of the beads so the row is next to the covered area (figure 8).

figure 8

- Continue the Backstitch as usual.

12 Fill in remaining areas using the Backstitch and the 11° beads (figure 9). Review the surface of the bead-work. Add 11° beads to cover any open spots.

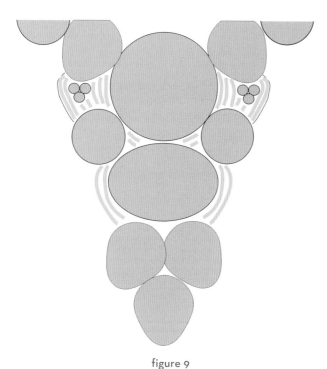

figure 9

13 The next steps are to trim and add an edge; however, the neck sides indicate a problem. The V shape between focals is so deep that there isn't room for edge beads on each side. Stitch a bead or two at the intersection of the focals on both sides (figure 10). This will smooth out the line of the edge and allow for a complete and attractive edge row.

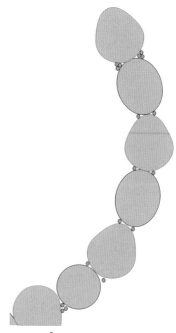

figure 10

14 The back collar sections look great when lying flat, but when worn as a necklace, they will be bent over the shoulder and around the back. When that section is bent, the rows separate and expose the backing. To compensate for this, add a string of beads at each of these areas. Stitch up three beads from the intersection on the partial additional row. Stitch through those three beads. Pick up three or more 11° beads to fill and loop over to the other side of the additional row. Stitch through three beads on that side and down through the backing (figure 11). Repeat for each intersection on the necklace.

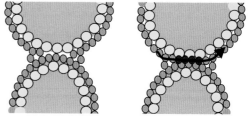

figure 11

15 Trim the backing. Apply the outer-backing and trim. Use the 11° beads and stitch the edge with the Clean Edge with one exception: at the back ends, switch to the Sunshine Edge for five beads, and then continue using the Clean Edge to finish.

16 Use the 11° beads and create a Herringbone Loop Attachment—Sideways Loop Variation, nine beads tall into the Sunshine Edge beads at the back ends. Use the jump rings to attach the hook and chain.

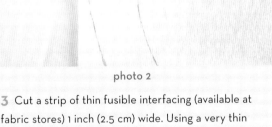

Joining Pieces of Backing

This collar pattern is larger than a standard-size backing sheet, but you can join pieces to make a larger piece. This is also useful when you are creating something and a design change requires you to have a larger backing than you originally cut.

1 Determine the place to enlarge and cut a straight line in that spot (photo 1).

photo 1

2 Cut an additional piece of backing with a straight line. Position it next to the area you need to enlarge.

photo 2

3 Cut a strip of thin fusible interfacing (available at fabric stores) 1 inch (2.5 cm) wide. Using a very thin layer of glue that dries flexible, glue the strip over the area you want to enlarge and let it dry.

4 Use a Whipstitch to stitch over the edges of the interfacing and at the intersection of the pieces (photo 2).

Circulating
Round
Necklace

What You Need

10 silver leaf jasper puffed flat round beads, 30 mm

8 bronzite puffed flat round beads, 16 mm

10 bronzite round beads, 6 mm

Three 15-inch (38.1 cm) strands of freshwater rice pearls, gold, 4 mm

10 pieces each of backing and outer-backing, 2 x 2 inches (5.1 x 5.1 cm)

Standard Necklace Kit Using Thread (page 15)

Standard Beading Kit (page 14)

Seed Beads

    8 grams of 15° dark bronze metallic

    15 grams of 11° dark brown opaque matte

What You Do

1 For each 30-mm round: Glue onto a piece of backing and let it dry. Sew on with the One-Bead Stitch. Create a Standard/Plain Bezel using the pearls and Couch Stitch for the base row. Use the 15° beads for the bezel row. Stitch an additional row using the 11° beads. Trim the backing. Apply the outer-backing and trim it. Use the 11° beads and stitch the edge using the Sunshine Edge stitch. Find and mark the center top and bottom.

> **tip** When marking centers, decide which is the bead's top so you can manage the difference in view based on the pattern or chatoyance in the focal. Use a long-thread marking on the top and a short-thread marking on the bottom to avoid confusion later.

2 Arrange the components around the Neck Circle (page 12).

> **tip** Take time to play with your beads and your designs. You never know what grand idea will evolve from those adventures.

3 Use two or three connection points to Combine the front components as illustrated in figure 1. Read the lesson Combining Multiple Components (page 77).

figure 1

4 Use the 16-mm bead and Combine the three front sections (figure 2). Angle the bottom circles on each side toward the center and Combine them using two or three connection points (figure 3).

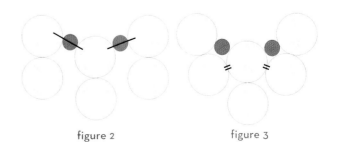

figure 2   figure 3

5 Connect the bottom sections as illustrated (figure 4). Use the 6-mm round and 11° beads as needed to span the distance.

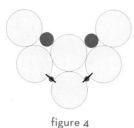

figure 4

6 Connect the pieces for the back of the collar, adding a 16-mm bead in between each component as illustrated (figure 5). The arrows in the illustration indicate the center tops and bottoms. Notice that the connection point is nearer the center top. Position so that all the edges of the circles for both components and 16-mm beads are near the Neck Circle line. For the ends, create a Herringbone Loop Attachment 16 beads tall using the 11° beads above a 16-mm bead.

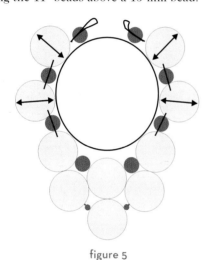

figure 5

> **tip** Try on pieces as you create. When recreating a project from a book, you see the end result before you complete the steps; this isn't the case when you are designing your own piece. It is helpful to try the necklace on and look in a mirror to get true feedback as you execute. You can continue with your original plan, or change directions. Try on this necklace. You may decide to add fringe, add more components, or just keep on with the original design.

7 Add drops below the 16-mm beads in the back (figure 6). Stitch though the fifth edge bead below the connection point and pick up seven 11°, one 6 mm, and one 11° as a turn bead. Stitch back through the 6 mm and pick up seven 11° beads. Stitch through the fifth edge bead below the connection point on the other side (figure 7). Stitch through the backings. Repeat the thread path twice to reinforce it.

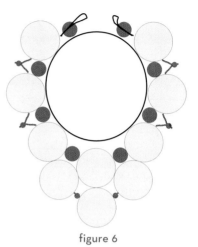

figure 6

> **tip** Use two connection points on necklaces or bracelets. The second connection point may be decorative (like in this project), but it also stabilizes the construction so the piece doesn't twist on a single connection point.

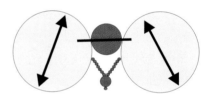

figure 7

8 Add the front embellishments (figure 8).

• For the near center on the right, exit the edge bead one down from the connection point. Pick up three 11°, one 6 mm, and one 11° for the turn bead. Stitch back through the 6 mm and pick up four 11° beads. Stitch through the edge bead one below the connection point on the other side. Repeat the thread path to reinforce it. Repeat for the left side in mirror image.

• For the connections to the side, exit on the sixth bead down from the connection point. Pick up four 11°, one 6 mm, and one 11° for the turn bead. Stitch back through the 6 mm and pick up four 11°. Stitch through the edge bead six below the connection point on the other side. Repeat the thread path to reinforce it. Repeat for the other side of the necklace.

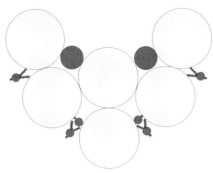

figure 8

9 On the bottom edge of each component, use the 15° beads and Pointed Edge Stitch.

10 Use the jump rings and attach the hook and chain.

Combining Multiple Components

1 Lay the components down on paper arranged as desired. Trace around each one.

2 Plan your stitching sequence based on which connections are most important. Connections are more important when they will determine the placement for other connections and are typically in the center of the finished piece. Use this sequence to complete the remaining steps.

3 For a combination area, identify the edge beads on one side of the combination. Stick a needle into the backing above one of the beads and note how many beads to use, and in which direction. Or, if the component has a center top and bottom marked, count the edge beads from that marking.

4 Pick up the component. Use a pen to mark the backing under those beads, putting a small dot under each edge bead.

5 Replace the component on the sheet and repeat the process above for the component on the other side of the combination.

6 Pick up the components and stitch them together. Use your common sense to determine how many edge beads to connect and how many times to stitch though the beads. These decisions will be affected by the components' sizes, weights, and whether or not they are in a position that is pulled, twisted, or generally stressed. You can use numerous connection points even if the edges don't touch. Simply fill in with other beads to extend the area as illustrated (below).

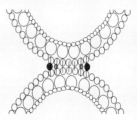

7 Replace the combined section on the paper and identify the next combination spot. Repeat steps 3 though 6 for all combination spots.

Indian Summer Necklace

Based on Circulating Round Necklace (page 74)

Key Elements: Red creek jasper teardrop bead, 20 x 25 mm; red creek jasper puffed oval bead, 25 x 36 mm; red creek jasper puffed round beads, 18 mm; tigereye puffed round beads, 12 mm; tigereye round tube beads, 12 x 4 mm; gray feldspar round beads, 6 mm

Necklace Strand: Tigereye flat beveled rectangle beads, 9 x 15 mm; gray feldspar round beads, 6 mm; Standard Necklace Instructions for Direct Attachment Sunshine Edge—Two Edge Beads (page 146)

Stitches/Techniques: Standard/Plain Bezel, Sunshine Edge, Fringe, Combining Multiple Components Lesson (page 77)

tip Using 4-mm beads in fringe will result in chunky fringe strands that hang over each other. Alternatives include alternating the fringe design using a 4 mm in one strand and then 11° beads in the next or using every other edge bead for the fringe. Another alternative (used in this necklace [figure 2]) is to utilize two edge beads for each fringe and use doubled thread. This will result in the fringe lying flat but will also give a solid appearance.

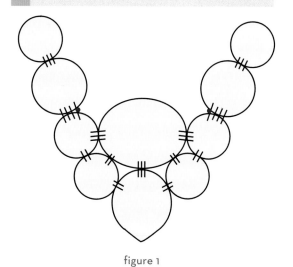

figure 1

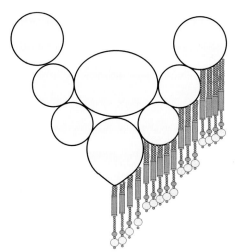

figure 2

Golden Circle Necklace

Based on Circulating Round Necklace (page 74)

Key Elements: Rivoli, crystal, 12 mm; crystal tear-drops, top drilled, 22 x 11 mm and 15 x 7.5 mm; crystal bicone beads, crystal AB, 3 mm and 4 mm; crystal round beads, 4 mm and 6 mm

Necklace Strand: Crystal round beads, 8 mm; Standard Necklace Instructions for Direct Attachment Sunshine Edge—Two Edge Beads (page 146)

Stitches/Techniques: Create a Flat Base Lesson (page 119), Standard/Plain Bezel (use 6° seed beads for the base row and 15° beads for the bezel row and an additional row), Sunshine Edge (use 11° beads), Side Petal Edge, Loops on Sunshine Edge Lesson (page 107)

> Use a very mild glue when gluing any foil-backed focals. The foil backing often interacts with glue and will ruin the appearance of the focal. Do one first to test.

Combine the columns and side components using the 6-mm beads on top and the 4-mm beads below. Identify the edge beads to use by counting up from the connection points as illustrated (figure 1). Skip the edge beads noted in pink. Mark the spots for the attachment of the necklace portion, counting above the connection point as illustrated in figure 1.

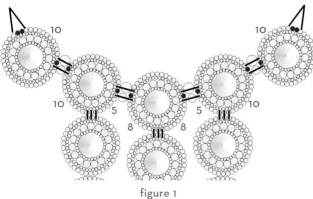

figure 1

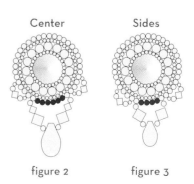

Center   Sides

figure 2   figure 3

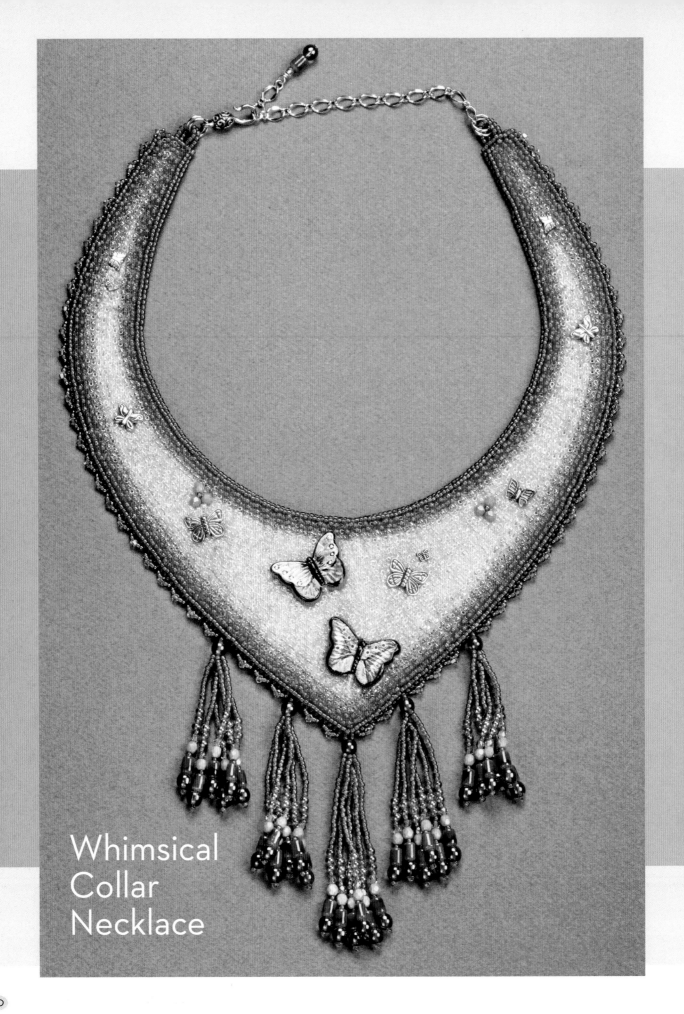

Whimsical
Collar
Necklace

What You Need

NOTE: The supplies list below details the beads used in this project as photographed, but it also identifies how the bead is used in the project so you can easily substitute beads from your collection, selecting your own colors.

Surface Decoration Beads

2 glass butterfly beads, hand painted, 20 x 18 mm

9 to 15 brass butterfly beads, various sizes from 4 x 4 mm to 14 x 10 mm

6 glass round beads, Picasso purple, 4 mm

Edge Decoration Beads, Side Petal Edge

62 to 68 crystal bicone beads, light rose, 3 mm

Tassel Beads

90 glass round beads, gold AB, 3 mm

30 glass round beads, Picasso purple transparent, 6 mm

5 glass round beads, Picasso purple transparent, 6 mm (topper above tassel)

30 glass round beads, Picasso purple opaque, 4 mm

30 fire-polished glass round beads, hot pink, 3 mm

30 cat's-eye glass tube beads, purple, 6 x 4 mm

1 piece each of backing and outer-backing, 8½ x 11 inches (21.6 x 27.9 cm)

Standard Necklace Kit Using Thread (page 15)

Standard Beading Kit (page 14)

Seed Beads

Use five shades from dark to light of any color you desire, mixing bead finishes (such as matte, color-lined, luster, transparent, etc.) as desired.

5 grams of 15° dark purple transparent AB

20 grams of 11° dark purple color-lined (color 1)

15 grams of 11° fuchsia pink color-lined (color 2)

10 grams of 11° dark pink transparent AB (color 3)

10 grams of 11° medium pink transparent AB (color 4)

15 grams of 11° pale pink transparent AB (color 5)

What You Do

1 Create a Collar Form as described on page 13 through step 3. Mark ⅜ inch (9.5 mm) out at the collar ends (A). Mark 1 inch (2.5 cm) out halfway down the neck (B). Mark 3 inches (7.6 cm) down at the center bottom (C). Mark 1¾ inches (4.4 cm) down at the center bottom and then 1½ inches (3.8 cm) out from there (D) (figure 1). Draw a curve, connecting the marks (figure 2). Fold the paper in half, and cut it out to create the pattern. Try it on. Make any needed adjustments for fit or to change the shape as desired.

2 Trace the pattern onto the backing and cut it out. Mark the center front line carefully, using a light color pen.

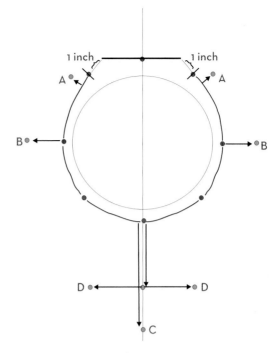

figure 1

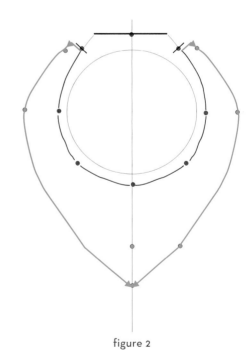

figure 2

3 Stitch a row of Backstitch around the entire edge using the dark purple (color 1) seed beads.

4 Stitch two rows of Picot Stitch next to the row of Backstitch using fuchsia pink (color 2) seed beads.

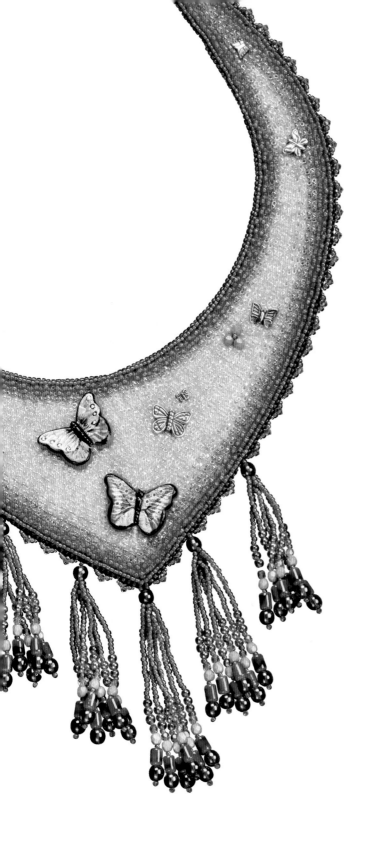

5 Use the surface decoration beads and arrange them on the collar. Put large focals in front and space clusters throughout (figure 10). Move them around until

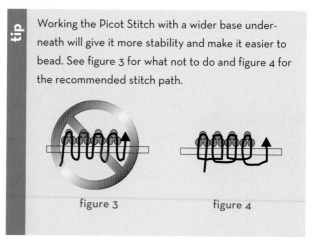
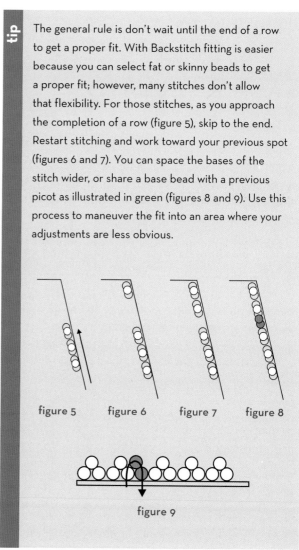

you have an arrangement you like. Glue the beads down and let them dry. Sew the beads on using the One-Bead Stitch.

6 Using dark pink (color 3) beads, stitch a row of Picot Stitch next to the previous rows. Stitch another row

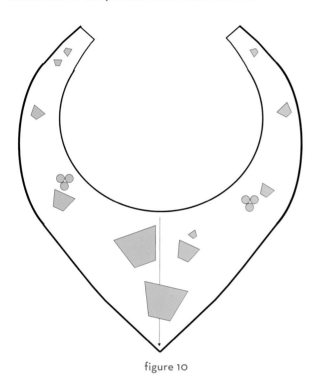

figure 10

with color 3 on the bottom only. Repeat using medium pink transparent AB (color 4).

7 Fill the remaining area with pale pink transparent AB (color 5), following the instructions in the lesson Filling with Picot Stitch (page 56).

8 Apply the outer-backing and trim. Stitch the edge using color 1 beads. On the inside curve of the collar, use the Clean Edge and finish the rest with the Sunshine Edge stitch.

9 Using color 1 beads and the Herringbone Loop Attachment—Sideways Loop Variation, create loops at the back edge 10 beads tall. Attach the hook and chain with jump rings.

10 Read the lesson Create a Tassel (page 84) to create a six-strand tassle. The topper is comprised of one 6-mm round and one 11°. The end sequence is three 3-mm gold, one 11°, one 3-mm hot pink, one 4-mm purple, one 11°, one tube, one 6-mm round, and an 11° turn bead. Use a count of 23 for the bottom tassel

and attach to the center bottom. If the center bottom is between two beads, use another 11° in the topper, one on each side. Use a count of 18 for the side middle tassels and attach into the eleventh edge bead from the center bottom. Use a count of 14 for the far side tassels and attach into the sixteenth edge bead above the previous tassel.

11 Finish the bottom edge with the Side Petal Edge using the 3-mm purple, 15°, and 11° beads. Start at the bottom center and work up one side. Do two side petals and skip to the other side of the next tassel. Do three side petals and skip to the other side of the tassel. Finish with petals over the rest of the edge. The spaces illustrated in green (figure 11) give room for the tassels to hang properly. Repeat for the other side.

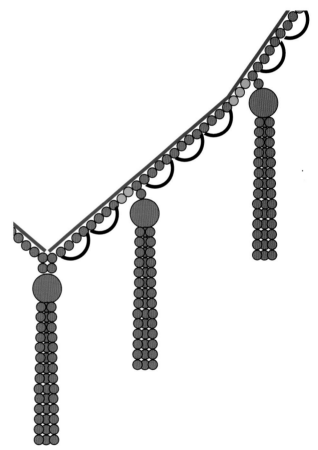

figure 11

Create a Tassel

The fringes on a tassel consist of a count of seed beads (typically 11° beads), the end sequence (typically larger beads), and a turn bead (usually an 11° bead).

figure 12

1 Use 2 yards (1.8 m) of single thread with a stop bead and a 9-inch (22.9 cm) tail.

2 Pick up five 11° seed beads and stitch through the first three beads again to create a loop (figure 12).

3 Pick up the count of seed beads, the end sequence, and the turn bead. Skip the turn bead and stitch back through the added beads plus the loop bead (figure 13). Repeat for the other side (figure 14).

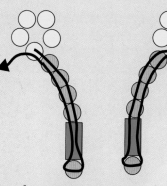

figure 13

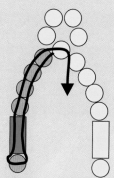

figure 14

4 For a six-strand tassel, skip this step. For a seven-strand tassel, pick up the count of seed beads, the end sequence, and the turn bead. Skip the turn bead and stitch through the added beads and the bead in the loop, entering at the other side (figure 15).

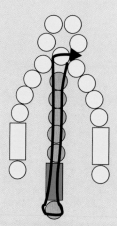

figure 15

5 Stitch around the loop beads to the other side (figure 16). Pick up the count of seed beads, the end sequence, and the turn bead. Skip the turn bead and stitch back through the added beads plus the bead in the loop. Stitch around the loop to the other side (figure 17). Pick up the count of seed beads, the end sequence, and the turn bead. Skip the turn bead and stitch back through the added beads plus the top loop bead (figure 18).

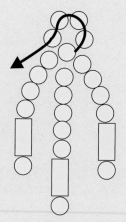

figure 16

6 Put a needle on the tail thread. Stitch up into the topper bead(s) and into the edge bead, staying on the top side. Stitch under the beads there and through the backings to the back side at least ¼ inch (6 mm) from the edge. Stitch back out through the edge bead, down the topper bead(s), and through two of the loop beads. Repeat this with the

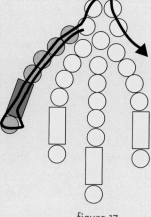

figure 17

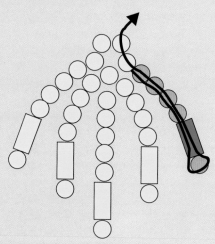

figure 18

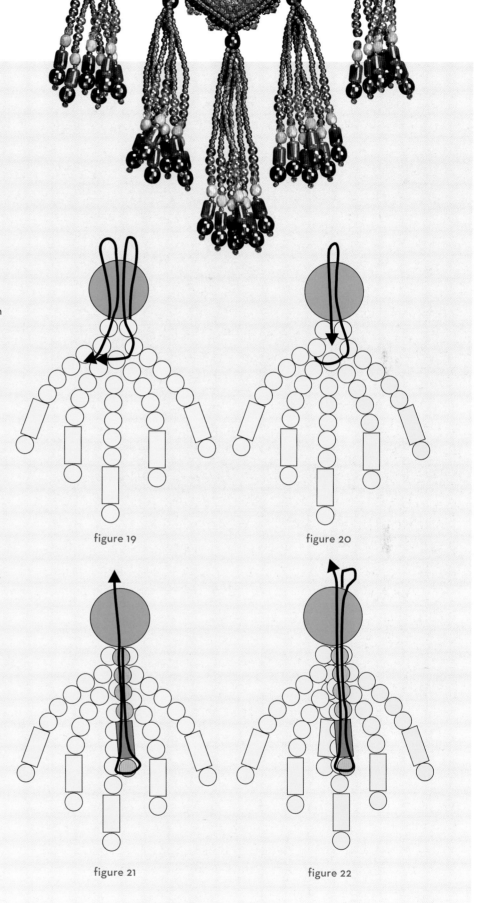

needle thread, stitching into the two loop beads on the other side, plus the bottom loop bead, so the threads are next to each other (figure 19). Tie a square knot twice. Use the needle thread and stitch around the loop.

7 Stitch up into the topper bead(s) and into the edge bead, staying on the top side. Stitch under the beads there and through the backings to the back side at least ¼ inch (6 mm) from the edge. Stitch back out through the edge bead and down the topper bead(s) on the front side of the loop (figure 20). Pick up the count of seed beads, the end sequence, and the turn bead. Skip the turn bead and stitch back through the added beads (figure 21).

8 Repeat step 7, except put the new fringe on the back side of the loop (figure 22). Stitch up the topper bead(s) through the backings as before and down through the topper bead(s). Stitch into the top two loop beads on the side opposite where the tail thread is.

9 Take the tail thread and stitch over to the needle thread. Tie a square knot twice. Weave the ends into the fringes and cut them.

figure 19

figure 20

figure 21

figure 22

Vegas
Vacation
Necklace

What You Need

4 buttons, shank type, playing cards, one of each suit, 15 x 20 mm

1 black onyx round cabochon, 8-mm thick cut, 20 mm in diameter

1 black onyx round cabochon, 6-mm thick cut, 15 mm in diameter

11 glass flat round black-and-white bull's-eye beads, 10 mm

3 glass shoe-shaped drops, black with white, 10 x 15 mm

1 glass shoe-shaped drop, white with black, 10 x 15 mm

1 glass playing-card drop, white with black, 9 x 14 mm

1 glass playing-card drop, black with white, 9 x 14 mm

2 glass domino drops, black with white, 7 x 13 mm

2 mother-of-pearl square beads, white with black stripes, 12 mm

2 glass triangle beads, top drilled, black opaque, 8 x 12 mm

80 to 100 glass round beads, black opaque, 4 mm

40 to 50 acrylic dice beads, corner cut, black, 6 mm

80 to 100 acrylic dice beads, corner cut, white, 6 mm

1 piece each of backing and outer-backing, 8½ x 11 inches (21.6 x 27.9 cm)

1 piece each of backing and outer-backing, 5 x 5 inches (12.7 x 12.7 cm)

2 ounces (56 grams) of air-dry clay

Standard Necklace Kit Using Thread (page 15)

Standard Beading Kit (page 14)

Seed Beads

    20 grams of 15° white opaque

    2 grams of 15° red opaque

    50 grams of 11° white opaque

    5 grams of 11° black opaque

    2 grams of 8° black opaque

    5 grams of 6° black opaque

    5 grams of bugle beads, black opaque, 7 mm

What You Do

1 Mark a center line and several horizontal lines on the 5 x 5-inch (12.7 x 12.7 cm) piece of backing.

2 Center the 20-mm cabochon 1½ inches (3.8 cm) from the bottom edge of the backing. Glue it on and let it dry. Create a Standard/Plain Bezel using the 6° beads for the base row and the 15° white beads for the bezel row.

3 Position the bull's-eye beads below the cabochon with the top two touching the base row and the bottom one touching the top two. Glue them on and let them dry. Sew on with the One-Bead Stitch. Stitch around the grouping with the Backstitch using the 8° beads.

4 Position and stitch on the buttons. First create a donut shape around the shank using air-dry clay and let it dry; this will keep the buttons level. Glue the donut on, and stitch the button through the hole (figures 1 and 2).

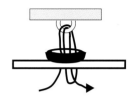

figure 1   figure 2

5 Use the 6° and 11° black beads with the Stacks Stitch and stitch around each button. Position the stack so the turn bead touches the side of the button and the 6° bead is partially under the button (figure 3). Although the button will be stable from the donut above, this further stabilizes it and provides an attractive edge to hide the underside.

figure 3

6 Position the 15-mm cabochon above the cards, glue it down, and let it dry (figure 4). Create a Standard/Plain Bezel using the 8° beads for the base row and the 15° white beads for the bezel row.

figure 4

7 Draw curved lines from under the cards to the bull's-eye beads (figure 5). Use the 11° white beads and stitch a row of Backstitch along those lines and around the other focals.

figure 5

8 Fill in with Backstitch using the 11° white beads (figure 6). Trim the backing. Apply the outer-backing and trim it. Use the 11° white beads and stitch the edge with the Sunshine Edge stitch.

figure 6

9 Read the lesson Construction for a Cutout (page 91).

10 Create a Collar Form (page 13) through step 3. Mark ½ inch (1.3 cm) out at the collar ends (A). Mark 1 inch (2.5 cm) out halfway down the neck (B). Mark 2 inches (5.1 cm) down at the center bottom (C). Mark 1½ inches (3.8 cm) out between the 1-inch (2.5 cm) and 2-inch (5.1 cm) marks (D) (figure 7). Draw a curve, connecting these marks (figure 8). Position the completed beadwork in the desired location and adjust your Collar Form, if desired. Once you have the position and collar shape you like, mark ⅜ inch (9.5 mm) around the edge of the completed beadwork (photo 1). Fold the Collar

Form in half and cut it out to create your pattern. Place the pattern on the backing and trace. Leave the cutout area and cut the rest of the outline (see tip, bottom left, next page).

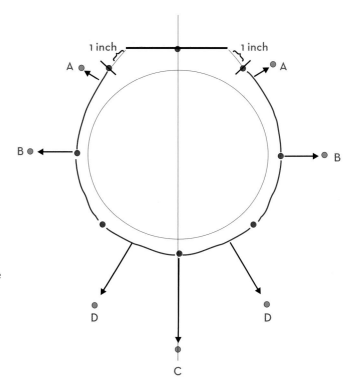

figure 7

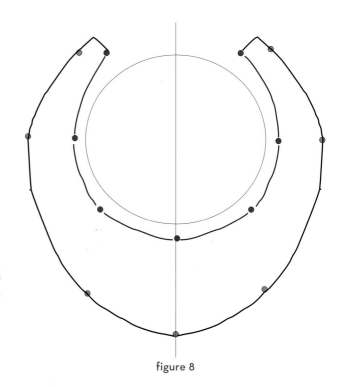

figure 8

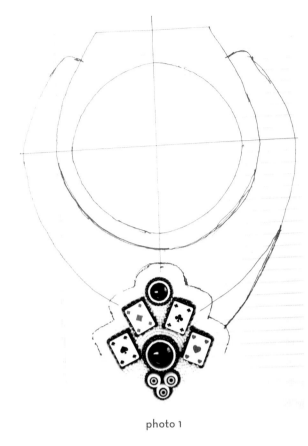

photo 1

11 Stitch a row of Backstitch around the outside edge. Use the 11° black around the cutout area and the 11° white for the rest. Add a row of Picot Stitch around the cutout area using the 11° white beads for the base and the 11° black beads at the center top of the picot. Use this row to push the Backstitch row into proper position.

12 Use the shoe, playing card, dominos, triangle, bulls-eye, and mother-of-pearl beads and drops, referring to figure 9 for the placement. Glue them on and let them dry. Stitch beads on with the One-Bead Stitch. Use the Stacks Stitch for the drops as illustrated in the Tip, below.

tip When reinforcing a Stacks Stitch, don't just repeat the thread path because there is not enough base underneath to anchor the stitch. Instead, create a stitch over to one side, and then repeat the thread path. This process can be done numerous times if desired.

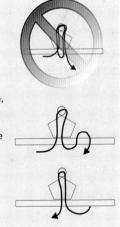

13 Use the Lazy Stitch with an 11° black, a bugle, and an 11° black to create bugle rows positioned as illustrated in red (figure 9, next page). Create a row of Backstitch around the other focals using the 11° beads; use black around white focals and white around black focals.

tip Often a completed piece of beadwork is not exactly symmetrical. When you trace the outline for a cutout, you can either fold the paper in half and cut it out so the border is symmetrical (the option chosen here) or you can cut the outline as drawn, then fold and cut the rest of the pattern—designer's choice. This will affect how the cutout sits inside the border.

tip As a general rule, I recommend cutting the backing first and then beading so you get a good shape without cutting any threads. In this case, however, if the cutout area was precut, then there would be only a thin strip connecting the collar sides. Common sense said to leave that area uncut and use care with stitch placement and when trimming that area later.

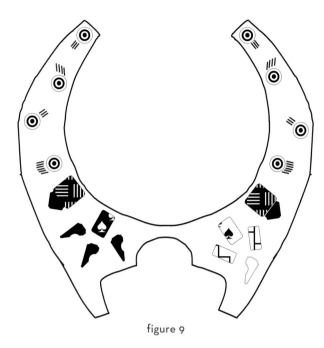

figure 9

14 Fill the remaining area with Backstitch as illustrated in figure 10 using the 11° white beads. Review the surface area and stitch beads into gaps using thick and thin beads, turning any direction as needed. Use the 15° white beads for small areas.

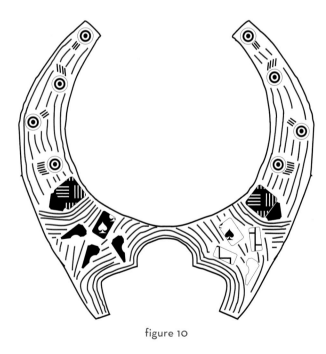

figure 10

15 Trim the cutout area. Apply the outer-backing and trim. Use the 11° white beads and stitch the edge using the Sunshine Edge stitch.

16 The Fringe Edge on the centerpiece is branch fringe using the 15° white, 15° red, 4-mm, white dice, and black dice beads. The 15° red beads are used for the turn bead on the bottom. The 15° white is used for the core, the branches, and the turn bead on the branches. Find the center bottom. For the first fringe, pick up a core of 35, one 4-mm, one white dice, and a red turn bead. Stitch back up eight beads into the core and create a branch of five beads, one black dice, and a white turn bead. Repeat this for two more fringes on each side, except alternate the dice colors on the bottom and fringe. Continue adding fringes, alternating the colors and reducing the core by one. Add fringes on the bottom of the curve only—not up the sides. See the area with the red arrow in figure 11.

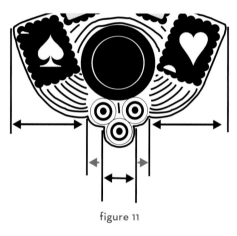

figure 11

17 The next section is noted in green in figure 11. Start with a core of 35 and the same fringe design as in step 16. Reduce the count of the core by one for the next fringes and alternate the dice colors. This is a small section with only three or four fringes; do not fringe up the curved side.

18 The final section is noted in blue in figure 11. Start with a core of 33 and the same fringe design as in step 16. Reduce the count of the core by one for the next fringes and alternate the dice colors. Stop adding the branch as the curve turns upward, after 10 to 12 fringes. When there are 12 fringes left to do, stop adding the 4-mm bead and add four to the current count of core beads, then continue to reduce by one. When there are four edge beads left, share the fringe using two edge beads for one fringe.

19 Place the center piece into the collar section and determine the connection points. Use the 4-mm round beads between them and Combine at each connection point, noted in yellow in figure 12.

figure 12

20 Stitch an edge around the collar using the 15° white, 15° red, white dice, and 4-mm round beads (figure 13). Use doubled thread and stitch into the backings before each dice section. Don't just loop around the edge beads because that is not secure enough.

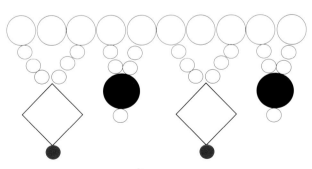

figure 13

21 Use the 11° white beads and create a Herringbone Loop Attachment—Sideways Loop Variation 10 beads tall at the ends of the collar. Use jump rings to attach the hook and chain on the loops.

Construction for a Cutout

Cutouts are an interesting design choice. Using them is similar to combining except that you create parallel edges and Combine with a few beads in between, leaving an open area.

1 Create one of the pieces all the way through the edge beading.

2 Decide which beads to use to attach and note the size of the bead. Use a ruler and measure the width of the bead plus the width of an edge bead (typically an 11°). When using a 4-mm bead to Combine on an edge of 11° beads, ³⁄₈ inch (9.5 mm) is a good approximation.

3 Place the beaded piece on the backing of the other piece. Position it where you want it to be after it is attached. Trace a line around it, adding the measurement in step 2 above. Cut on that line as the edge of the other piece.

4 Bead the other piece through the edge beading.

5 Combine the two pieces using the beads chosen in step 2. Use your common sense for the number of attachment points and how many times to stitch to reinforce. This will depend on weight, size, and how much pulling or stress the connection points have.

The process for a cutout is the same whether you are doing one or multiple cutouts on the edge, or a cutout in the center.

CHAPTER 6

Asymmetrical Necklaces

*Asymmetrical designs have right and left sides that are different, not mirror images.
While the design is different on each side, the main objective is to have balance.
There needs to be a balance of weight so that the necklace will stay centered when
worn, and there should also be a visual balance for eye appeal.*

You can adjust the physical weight of one side versus the other by using different materials in the beadwork. Find materials that are lighter than typical components (such as shells, Lucite, or hollow beads) when you need to lighten one side. Likewise, materials that are heavier like magnesite, hematite, and pyrite can be used to add weight. When you pick up a component that is lighter or heavier than you expect, check to see what material was used to make the component. Store that information for future reference to help with asymmetrical designs.

Unfortunately, there isn't a formula that will ensure visual balance. Instead, it's just one of those things where "you know it when you see it." As a general rule, construct the design so that the area on one side is roughly equivalent to the total area on the other side.

Use this as your starting point, and then just use your judgment (and your eyes) from there. When designing asymmetrical pieces, it's even more important to be critical to make sure the design works. Be willing to change your design as needed if it doesn't.

The following projects include the processes I used to create the designs so that you can not only create the exact project but also fashion your own asymmetrical design.

Sea-Foam Splendor Necklace

What You Need

3 new jade puffed flat square beads, sea green, 20 mm

2 new jade puffed flat round beads, sea green, 15 mm

5 new jade puffed flat oval beads, sea green, 12 x 16 mm

30 to 35 new jade faceted round beads, sea green, 8 mm

150 to 175 new jade round beads, sea green, 4 mm

3 pieces each of backing and outer-backing, 1½ x 1½ inches (3.8 x 3.8 cm)

7 pieces each of backing and outer-backing, 1¼ x 1¼ inches (3.2 x 3.2 cm)

Standard Necklace Kit Using Thread (page 15)

Standard Beading Kit (page 14)

Seed Beads

   5 grams of 15° ice green shimmering

   1 gram of 15° topaz/pale green color-lined

   18 grams of 11° topaz/pale green color-lined

   8 grams of 8° eggshell opaque

What You Do

1 Start by creating a symmetrical background shape, in this case a bib shape. Use the Neck Form Page (page 12) and begin by marking ½ inch (1.3 cm) below the neckline on the bottom half. Mark ½ inch (1.3 cm) in from the neck sides and 2 inches (5.1 cm) down the center. Connect with a curve. Fold the page in half and cut out the bib shape. Place it on another Neck Form Page and trace it. We'll refer to this as the *bib form page*.

> **tip** Sometimes you start with the bib shape and fit the focals into it. You can also start with a collection of focals. Place the focals on the Neck Form Page, move them around, add more, or remove some. Do this to help determine the shape of the bib: rounded, pointed, thin, or long. Once you've decided the basic bib shape, draw it and fit the focals into it. Small components help with fit issues.

2 Bead the components for your bib. Use the 1½-inch (3.8 cm) square backings and glue the square beads onto them. Glue the other beads onto the other backing pieces. Let them dry. For each: Sew on with the One-Bead stitch. Create a Standard/Plain Bezel using the 8° beads for the base row and the 15° shimmer beads for the bezel row. Trim the backing. Apply the outer-backing and trim. Stitch the edge with the 11° beads using the Sunshine Edge stitch. Leave the needle threads to use later. Weave in and cut the tail threads.

3 Place the beaded components on the bib form page. Use the larger components first and fill in with the rest. Move them around until you have an arrangement you like. You can have all sides touching or plan to put beads in between when combining. Photo 1 shows the two bib shapes that were considered during the design process.

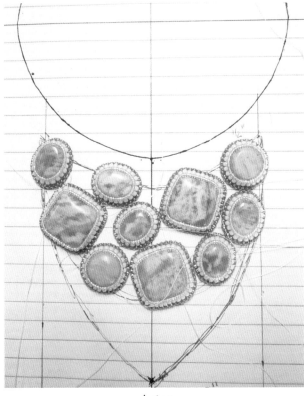

photo 1

4 Read the lesson Combining Multiple Components on page 77 and perform the steps. Begin to Combine by stitching the combination points in the center and working outward and up.

5 Once all your combination areas are stitched, hold up the piece to judge its stability. Adjust as needed.

6 Add in other beads for design purposes. Fill unwanted gaps and balance colors. Use the 15° color lined and 4-mm beads. (See figure 1.)

7 The fringe for this piece is branch fringe with a rounded line on the bottom. Read the lesson Creating Fringe from an Uneven Edge (page 96) and do steps 1 and 2. Identify the beads at the center bottom and the top sides where the necklace portion will be attached (noted in red in figure 2). Use the shimmer beads for the 15° beads. Use the 11° beads for the core with an end sequence of a 4-mm bead and a 15° turn bead. The branch is six 15° beads, one 4-mm, and a 15° turn bead. Start at the center bottom. Pick up a count of core beads to reach the line and pick up the end sequence. Stitch back up into the core through five seed beads and create the first branch. Create a second branch four beads up the core. Repeat this approximately 1 inch (2.5 cm) on each side of the center. The next fringes have only one branch. Pick up a count of core beads to reach the line and pick up the end sequence. Stitch back up into the core through nine seed beads and create a branch. For the next fringe, stitch up into the core five beads and create the branch. Alternate these two placements of the branch for approximately 2 inches (5.1 cm). For the next section, alternate a fringe with no branch and a fringe with one branch up into the core through five seed beads. For the final section there are no branches. Stop before the beads for the necklace attachment.

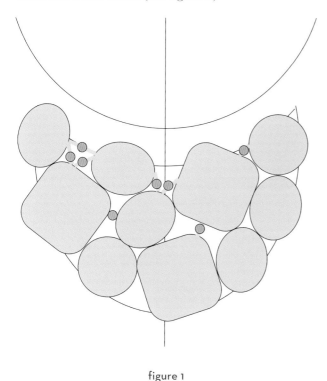

figure 1

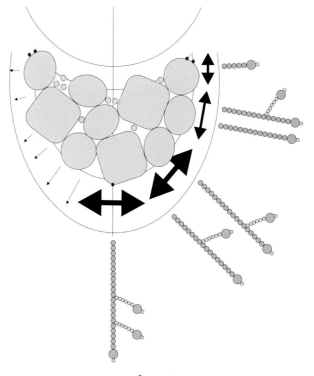

figure 2

8 Use the Standard Necklace Instructions for Direct Attachment Sunshine Edge—Two Edge Beads (page 146) with the 8-mm and 11° beads.

9 Use the 15° shimmer beads and finish the top edge with the Pointed Edge Stitch. If desired, stitch points in the open areas inside the bib surface.

lesson

Creating Fringe from an Uneven Edge

You can bead a smooth edge on the fringe bottom even if the edge you are fringing from is uneven.

1 Place the beadwork to be fringed on a piece of paper and trace it.

2 Draw a line below it where you want the fringe to end. If you are using an end sequence, draw a line above the previous line that represents where the end sequence starts.

3 Set the beadwork on the traced area and pick up the number of beads needed to reach the line(s).

4 As a general rule, reach the line by extending the thread straight down, as the fringe will hang on the body due to gravity. However, there are instances where gravity has less impact. One is short fringe when the fringe is not heavy. Another is branch fringe, because the bulk below tends to hold up the fringes above. When you have those instances, pick up beads radiating out to the line instead of straight down.

Waterfall Necklace

What You Need

1 chalk turquoise puffed flat round bead, 20 mm

1 chalk turquoise puffed flat teardrop bead, 20 x 35 mm

2 chalk turquoise puffed flat round beads, 15 mm

4 chalk turquoise puffed flat round beads, 10 mm

36-inch (91.4 cm) strand of turquoise chips, medium size

22 chalk turquoise oval beads, 8 x 10 mm

1 piece each of backing and outer-backing, 3 x 2½ inches (7.6 x 6.4 cm)

1 piece each of backing and outer-backing, 2¼ x 2¼ inches (5.7 x 5.7 cm)

6 pieces each of backing and outer-backing, 2 x 2 inches (5.1 x 5.1 cm)

Standard Necklace Kit Using Thread (page 15)

Standard Beading Kit (page 14)

Seed Beads

> 3 grams of 15° silver metallic
>
> 2 grams of 11° silver metallic
>
> 15 grams of 11° turquoise color-lined
>
> 2 grams of 8° turquoise opaque
>
> 5 grams of 6° turquoise opaque matte

What You Do

1 Match each of the chalk turquoise beads with a piece of appropriately sized backing. Glue them on and let them dry. Sew each one on with the One-Bead Stitch.

2 Create a Standard/Plain Bezel for each chalk turquoise bead. For the 10-mm round beads, use the 8° beads for the base row. For the others, use the 6° beads for the base row. For all: Use the 15° beads for the bezel row. Stitch an additional row using the 11° turquoise beads. Trim the backing. Apply the outer-backing and trim. Stitch the edge using the 11° turquoise beads and the Sunshine Edge stitch.

3 Use the Neck Form Page (page 12) and arrange the components as illustrated (figures 1 and 2; photo 1), or create your own design. Trace and Combine the components after reading the lesson Combining Multiple Components (page 77).

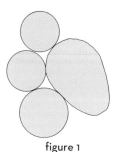

figure 1   figure 2

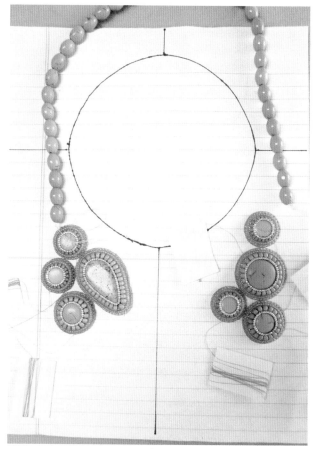

photo 1

 Note that the total area for each side is roughly the same. This is what makes the design work because it creates a visual balance, and the weight on each side is approximately equal, so it will hang as desired.

4 Attach the back strand of the necklace using the Standard Necklace Instructions for Direct Attachment Sunshine Edge—Two Edge Beads (page 146). Note that the right-hand side sits higher on the neck than the left. Use 11 oval beads on the left and 10 oval beads on the right, alternating each oval bead with the 11° silver beads.

5 The beadwork is now ready for the center multi-strands. The easiest way to proceed is to hang the piece on a neck display form (photo 2). This provides for immediate and accurate feedback about how gravity is affecting the design. You also can use the Neck Form Page (page 12); just be sure to pick up the necklace periodically to check the effect of gravity.

photo 2

6 The center strands use the chip beads and 11° turquoise beads. The design is at least five 11° beads from the edge bead, then a pattern of a chip and three 11° is repeated across the strand, ending with at least five 11° beads. Read the lesson Multistrand Connections (page 100) and see figure 3.

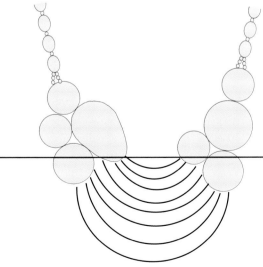

figure 3

Multistrand Connections

The general rule is to create the top strand first and continue to the bottom. After beading a few strands, stop and plan the position of all subsequent strands by putting a needle in each edge-bead connection point. When you are satisfied with the placements, mark the back side with a pen just under the edge beads selected and remove the needles.

1 Begin by identifying the edge beads on each side to use for the top strand. Picture a horizontal line from one side to the other to help decide which edge beads to use. Use doubled thread and stitch out though one of those edge beads.

2 Pick up beads for the strand, stitch over to the other side, and enter the edge bead, staying to the back side. Stitch through the backings to the top side at least ¼ inch (6 mm) from the edge.

3 Stitch over to the next edge bead that will have a strand, positioning the thread between and under beads on the top side. If the distance to that bead is long (more than ³⁄₁₆ inch [5 mm]) or you can't stitch to it directly (because of corners or a different component), then use the Running Stitch to travel to it. On the top side, use a longer stitch hidden between beads.

4 When you reach the next edge bead that will have a strand, stitch through the backings to the back side at least ¼ inch (6 mm) from the edge and stitch out the edge bead.

5 Repeat steps 2 through 4 for all of the strands. As you add strands, you will be adding weight to the center, which will pull the beading on the sides toward the center. Keep this in mind as you design. The first few strands will hang with a deeper curve on the bottom after the next strands are added.

Each strand in the Waterfall Necklace used the same beads and stringing pattern in each strand. However, you can use different beads in each strand or different stringing patterns for a variety of designs. If one strand will be significantly heavier than the other strands (usually because it has many larger beads), then add that strand first instead of following the general rule of adding strands from the top to the bottom. That way, you'll be able to see the impact gravity has on the design from the heavy strand and adjust the other strands more easily.

Royal Vines Necklace

What You Need

1 amethyst crystal formation, 20 to 30 mm

25 to 30 amethyst round beads, 8 mm

45 to 50 amethyst round beads, 6 mm

10 to 15 amethyst round beads, 4 mm

10 to 20 amethyst round beads, 2 mm

33 amethyst oval beads, 7 x 5 mm

3 to 10 amethyst bicone beads, 4 x 3 mm

1 amethyst faceted drop bead, top and side drilled, 7 x 6 mm

15 to 20 freshwater pearl rice beads, blue zircon, 5 mm

1 freshwater pearl round coin bead, blue zircon, 11 mm

1 freshwater pearl stick bead, long drilled, blue zircon, 12 mm

3 freshwater pearl stick beads, long drilled, olive green, 12 mm

25 to 40 peridot round beads, 7 mm

3 to 5 peridot round beads, 4 mm

10 to 20 peridot bicone beads, 4 x 3 mm

50 to 70 peridot rectangle beads, 3 x 4 mm

8 metal leaf drops, green, 20 x 28 mm

5 metal leaf drops, blue zircon, 20 x 28 mm

1 piece each of backing and outer-backing, 7 x 5 inches (17.8 x 12.7 cm)

Standard Necklace Kit Using Thread (page 15), plus 6 more jump rings and 1 three-strand gold metal drop finding

Standard Beading Kit (page 14)

Seed beads

    3 grams of 15° purple color-lined

    20 grams of 11° purple color-lined

    20 grams of 11° green metallic

    10 grams of 8° blue zircon transparent AB

    10 grams of 8° purple transparent AB

    2 grams of twisted bugle beads, transparent olive green rainbow, 12 mm

    2 grams of twisted bugle beads, purple metallic AB, 6 mm

What You Do

1 The pattern for this necklace is based on a symmetrical bib form. Use the Neck Form Page (page 12) and mark ¼ inch (6 mm) out from the neckline on the bottom half of the neck. Mark 1¼ inches (3.2 cm) down from the horizontal center on each side (A). Mark ¾ inch (1.9 cm) down from the center bottom (B) and an additional 2 inches (5.1 cm) below that (C). Just below the ¾-inch (1.9 cm) mark (B), mark out 2 inches

(5.1 cm) on each side (D). Connect the markings with curved lines (figure 1). Fold it in half and cut out the bib shape. Take the cutout bib shape and draw a line from left to right, near the center to the edge that roughly continues the downward curve of the neckline (figure 2). Cut on that line. Trim the upper left top, squaring it off. Trace it onto a Neck Form Page to create a bib form page (figure 3). Trace it onto the backing. Cut out the backing and mark the center line.

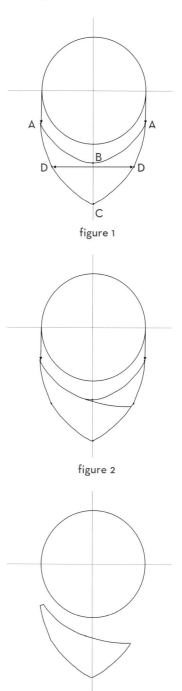

figure 1

figure 2

figure 3

2 Center the crystal on the bib, glue it down, and let it dry. Identify areas on the crystal where you can stitch a loop of beads over the crystal to secure its attachment to the backing (see figure 4). Each situation is different because each crystal is different; use your judgment based on the surface facets and the size of the crystal. The project has one loop using the 2-mm amethyst beads, which blend in and enhance the surface. Another loop was stitched on the other side using the 15° purple beads. Stitch as many loops as deemed necessary using any beads you find attractive.

figure 4

> **tip**
>
> If your crystal formation does not have a flat back, see the lesson Create a Flat Base (page 119). You can also increase the height or change the way it sits, lifting one side.

3 Typically, crystal formations are tall with an edge that drops sharply. Use beads of various sizes to sculpt around the formation to blend down to the base with a measured slope (figure 5). Start with large beads on the base and add beads on top of those as needed. Use the One-Bead Stitch and Stacks Stitch as needed. The beads surrounding the base for this project are 8-mm, 6-mm, and 4-mm rounds using the One-Bead Stitch. Bicone beads are used with the Stacks Stitch. The amethyst beads are used around the top and the peridot beads for a small section on the bottom (photos 1 and 2). Feel free to use your imagination.

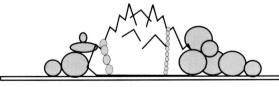

figure 5

photo 1

photo 2

4 The crystal in the center is the main focus. This design also includes three other clusters spread over the surface and a curved line that draws the eye across the area and spreads the color palette. Position and sew on the freshwater pearl sticks and coin using the One-Bead Stitch. Draw curved lines as illustrated and stitch over them using the 8° blue zircon beads and Backstitch (figure 6).

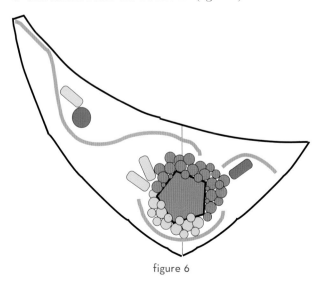

figure 6

5 Use Backstitch to fill the areas illustrated in figure 7. Use the 11° with colors matching the line colors and the 8° for the thick lines. Use the Lazy Stitch with the purple 11° and bugle beads and stitch them near the pearl coin. Fill the remaining open areas with the Picot Stitch using the 11° purple beads.

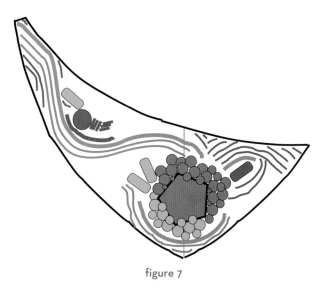

figure 7

6 Use the Stacks Stitch with the peridot bicones and 11° green for the turn bead and create stacks around the clusters noted in yellow in figure 8. Use the Stacks Stitch and 8° beads with 11° turn beads and create stacks noted in black in figure 8. Use the purple beads near the pearl coin and the blue zircon near the pearl stick on the right.

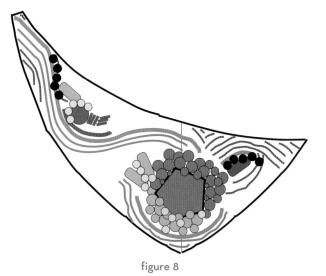

figure 8

7 Review and inspect the surface beading. Add beads to cover gaps and to add color or texture to areas as desired.

8 Apply the outer-backing and trim. Stitch the edge with the Sunshine Edge stitch. Use the purple and green 11° beads, switching colors on the edge to match the surface color changes.

9 Place the beaded bib on the bib form page created in step 1 and read the lesson Color and Texture Variety in Fringe (page 105). Draw a line from the center bottom up to the left where you want the fringe to extend to. Fold the paper in half, hold it up to the light, and duplicate that line on the right-hand side. Open it again and place the beadwork on the page. Space the leaf drops as desired (photo 3). Draw a line above the leaf tops. The leaf drops are not on every fringe, and the second line indicates the length of a fringe without a leaf drop (photo 4). Color as desired. Stitch the fringes according to the pattern created, using 11°, 8°, rectangle, round, and any other beads as desired.

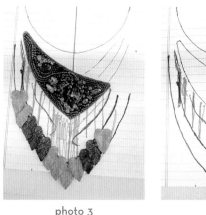 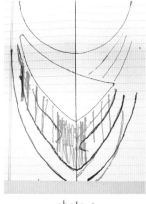

photo 3   photo 4

10 Place the beadwork on the bib form page. Use the Standard Necklace Instructions for Direct Attachment Sunshine Edge—Two Edge Beads (page 146) on the left-hand side. Use the 8-mm beads alternating with an 11° green bead circling around the neck, stopping ½ inch (1.3 cm) before the center line at the top (the back of the neck). This leaves room for the jump rings and hook.

11 Identify the edge beads you will use to attach the right-hand necklace strands by using your bib page and drawing lines that essentially fill in the area you cut off of the symmetrical bib form (see photo 4). Use the Standard Necklace Instructions for Direct Attachment Sunshine Edge—Single Edge Bead (page 145) and create the first strand using the amethyst 6-mm round and oval beads, alternating and separated with an 11° green bead. Create the inside strand first. Place the three-hole metal drop on the page at the back of the neck, positioned ½ inch (1.3 cm) from the center line on top. Create the length for the necklace near the metal drop, leaving room for the loop and jump rings. For the second and third strands, curve around the neck form and the previous strand(s). Each of the three strands on this project used the same count of beads; however, your sizing and execution may result in a different count.

tip Judging the length for each strand of a multi-strand necklace can be difficult. Use your Neck Form Page and start with the innermost strand. For subsequent strands, lay them around the previous strands, making them at least ¼ inch (6 mm) shorter than the previous strand. These need to be shorter because you are using a flat surface, which is not a true body shape. Create a beaded loop to end each strand and attach it to a finding with jump rings. Finish and try it on. You can adjust the length of the strands by adding jump rings or changing the size of the jump rings instead of remaking the strand.

lesson

Color and Texture Variety in Fringe

One method to create color changes in fringe is to count the beads and pick up different colors. This method works easily for geometric designs using one size of bead because it is easy to adjust the count and get the effect you desire. However, when you want to use varying sizes of beads in the fringe to add texture, this method is easier to perform.

1 Place the beadwork on a piece of paper and trace the outline.

2 Mark a line beneath to represent the end of the fringe length.

3 Use markers of various colors and color the fringe area. This is your pattern. Color in and draw lines—do whatever makes sense to signal the changes needed when beading.

4 Place the beadwork on the pattern as you work. Pick up beads of various sizes as desired and match the colors to the pattern underneath, changing the beads selected as the pattern changes.

5 Pull the thread straight down from the beadwork, the way the fringe will hang when worn to match to the pattern. Don't splay the fringe radiating out from the center.

CHAPTER 7

Earrings

No jewelry box is complete without earrings, and bead-embroidery techniques can be used to add fabulous creations to your earring wardrobe. These projects cover both wire and post-style earrings, all of which are for pierced ears. However, you can substitute clip-on ear findings, if desired, for nonpierced ears.

There are three critical considerations when designing earrings:

1 *The size of the earring.* This is listed first because bead embroiderers spend so much time making necklaces and bracelets that judging sizes and proportions for earrings can be difficult. Large earrings are wonderful; you just want to make sure the earrings won't be larger than desired. Draw a pattern or an outline of your design on paper, being sure to include space for bead rows and edges. Cut it out, hold it up to your ears, and look in a mirror to help you judge whether the final size and proportion are correct.

2 *The weight of the earring.* Earlobes are soft and can comfortably support only a limited amount of weight. There is not an exact weight limit because it is different for different people. Also, the weight limit can be increased by switching to a post-style finding instead of a wire-style finding. Dangling components increase the perception of weight because of the centrifugal force

when dangles move. Put all of the beads you intend to use in your palm. Feel their weight and choose between a post and a wire style, and potentially adjust your design as well. Performing this process and being aware of this issue in the design phase will help you avoid problems later.

3 *The edge treatment.* Do *not* use the raw Sunshine Edge row for your edge treatment. There are two reasons for this. First, earrings are worn near the face. A raw Sunshine Edge has exposed thread on the outside, which can easily be soiled by makeup. The second reason is that it is not attractive. This edge is often used for necklaces, but that edge is not exposed from the same angle as it is with an earring. Plus, how close up the piece is viewed is different. People will generally not put their faces next to your chest to look at your necklace (well, except at a bead show!), but they can easily see the exposed edge on earrings because their faces are on the same level. There are three solutions to finish the edge of an earring: the Sunshine Edge finished with another edge stitch, the Picot Variation of Sunshine Edge, or the Clean Edge.

Earring creation involves using finishing techniques to accommodate an earring finding. The two basic types of findings are wires and posts.

Wire Findings

Create a beaded loop to use to attach to the finding. Use pliers to open the loop on the finding, insert the beaded loop, and close it. There are different techniques to create a beaded loop, depending on the edge stitch used.

Loops on Sunshine Edge

1 Stitch from the back side to the front side at least ¼ inch (6 mm) from the edge. Stitch underneath the surface beadwork and out the edge bead. Pick up five to eight beads for the loop.

2 Stitch down into the other edge bead, staying on the top side. Stitch underneath the surface beadwork and down through the backings to the back side at least ¼ inch (6 mm) from the edge (figures 1 and 2).

3 Stitch out the edge bead and through the beads in the loop (figure 3).

4 Repeat steps 2 and 3 to reinforce and strengthen.

figure 1

figure 2

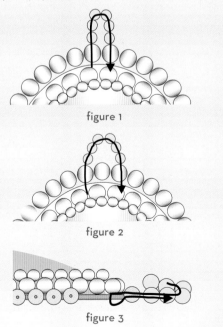

figure 3

Loops on Sunshine Edge–Picot Variation

1 From the back side, stitch through the backings to the top side at least ¼ inch (6 mm) from the edge and stitch out through the edge bead.

2 Stitch through the picot bead on top and pick up five to eight beads. Stitch through the top picot bead two beads over and down through the edge bead, staying on the top side (figure 4).

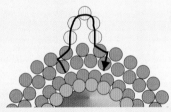

figure 4

3 Stitch through the backings to the back side at least ¼ inch (6 mm) from the edge. Stitch up through the edge bead (figure 5).

4 Repeat steps 2 and 3 without picking up the beads at least four more times to strengthen.

figure 5

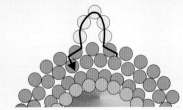

figure 6

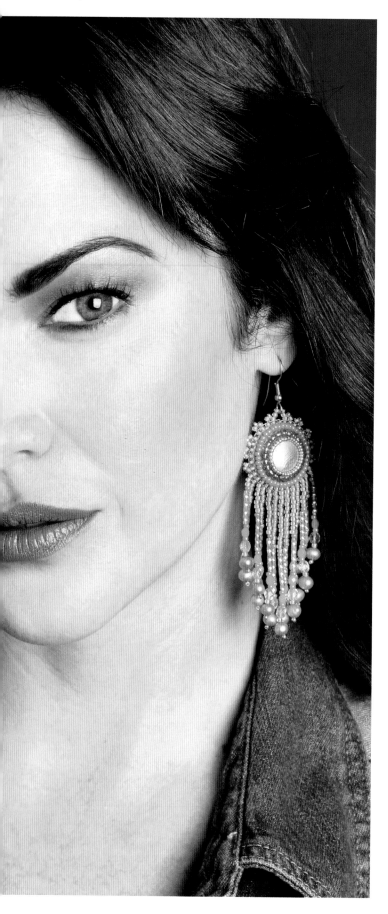

Loops on Clean Edge

1 Identify the edge beads to use for the attachment, shown in green in the illustration (figure 7). Stitch up from the back side to the top side on the outer edge of one of the edge beads. Stitch through the edge bead. Pick up five to eight beads for the loop. Stitch through the other edge bead.

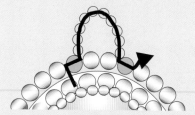

figure 7

2 Stitch through the backings from the top side to the back side at the outer edge of the edge bead and at least ¼ inch (6 mm) from the edge, positioned under the surface beadwork (figure 8).

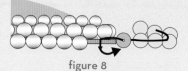

figure 8

3 Stitch through the edge bead, through the loop beads, and through the other edge bead (figure 9).

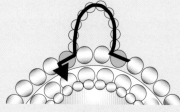

figure 9

4 Repeat steps 2 and 3 to reinforce and strengthen.

Post Findings

The post finding, adjusted as in the lesson that follows, is glued onto the backing surface, the outer-backing is applied, and then the edge is stitched.

Using Flashing with Findings

Findings include earring posts, pin findings, cuff-link findings, or any other finding that will be glued on. The critical issues to address are strength and stability. Using strong glue is not sufficient because you are gluing onto the backing, which is weak and can tear. To compensate for this, the backing area covered by the finding needs to be as large as possible to spread the stress. Use flashing to enlarge the area to be glued to the backing surface. Flashing, a thin metal used in roofing, is available at hardware stores and can be cut with tin snips or strong scissors. When the flashing covers the backing surface all the way to the edges, you also get stability added by the edge stitch, which sandwiches the flashing between the backing and the outer-backing.

1 Glue the finding to the flashing using an epoxy glue for metal.

2 Place the trimmed beadwork on a piece of paper and trace the outline (photo 1). Draw a line approximately ¼ inch (6 mm) inside the outline and cut on that line.

3 Lay the paper with the cutout hole over the flashing like a frame. Move it so the finding is in the position you desire and trace. Cut the flashing on the traced line (photo 2).

4 Glue the flashing-enlarged finding onto the backing.

photo 1   photo 2

Prepare flashing and findings in advance. Cut pieces of flashing and glue the findings on. Keep these in stock

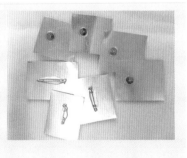

and ready to use when you want to create earrings or a pin.

Earring Design

As with the necklaces in this book, the earring projects start with "The One" and progress to more elaborate designs. You may want to review the design discussion and steps for pendant necklaces, starting on page 16, as these include concepts and steps that are also relevant to earring design. Likewise, the design discussion and steps for creating totem necklace designs (starting at page 36) also include information that's relevant to

earrings. The process of selecting beads, components, techniques, and colors are the same—just typically on a smaller scale. Just be sure to remember the other considerations discussed previously that are unique to earrings, such as weight and edge treatments.

Earring construction presents a new challenge because you are creating "two" instead of "one" and usually want them to match. In most instances, each earring is the same, or at least a mirror image of its mate. First, keep in mind that there is an organic look and feel to bead embroidery so an exact, every-single-bead match is not necessary. Don't overly stress about this issue; instead, identify where matching is important (like having the same size components or the same number of fringes), and pay special attention to those items in both the design and construction phases. Some people easily make one earring and then the other. Other people work both earrings simultaneously, completing each step first on one earring and then the other. Use whichever method is most comfortable and successful for you.

Whole Lotta Luv
Post Earrings

What You Need

2 white aventurine round cabochons, 20 mm

2 howlite flat heart beads, dyed blue, 6 mm

2 pieces each of backing and outer-backing, 1½ x 1½ inches (3.8 x 3.8 cm)

2 pieces of flashing, 1½ x 1½ inches (3.8 x 3.8 cm)

2 ear-post findings

Standard Beading Kit (page 14)

Seed Beads

    2 grams of 15° white ceylon

    3 grams of 11° white ceylon

    1 gram of 11° blue transparent

What You Do

1 Glue the cabochon onto the backing and let it dry. Create a Standard/Plain Bezel using the 11° white beads for the base row and the 15° beads for the bezel row.

2 Stitch up to the top side, positioning the needle on the cabochon edge and stitching up inside the bezel row. Pick up 15° beads, the heart bead, and 15° beads and lay the beads across the center of the cabochon. Adjust the counts of 15° beads as needed to span the distance to the bezel row on the opposite side, positioning the heart bead as desired. Stitch down to the back side, inside the bezel row and next to the cabochon edge. Repeat the thread path at least two more times to reinforce it.

3 Trim the backing and read the lesson Alternative Assembly Process (right).

4 Stitch the edge with the Sunshine Edge—Picot Variation using the 11° beads, alternating the colors as illustrated in figures 1 through 5.

5 Read the lesson Using Flashing with Findings (page 109) and do those steps, adjusting the size of the flashing according to step 3 of the lesson Alternative Assembly Process.

6 Apply the outer-backing and trim. Whipstitch it to the top picot bead on the edge.

7 Repeat steps 1 through 6 for the second earring.

lesson

Alternative Assembly Process

Usually, the backing is trimmed, the outer-backing is applied and trimmed, and then the edge beading stitches them together. What follows below is an alternative process. It can be used with any type of jewelry but is particularly advantageous for earrings and pins when you want to add a stabilizer that covers as much area as possible.

1 Perform the surface beading and trim the backing.

2 Stitch the edge on the backing only (do not add the outer-backing) using the Sunshine Edge—Picot Variation.

3 Add a stabilizer if desired. If you're creating earrings or a pin, the stabilizer is the flashing with the finding glued onto it. The stabilizer size can be just slightly larger than the under-backing shown as the red line in figure 6.

figure 6

4 Apply the outer-backing, cutting holes as needed to accommodate any findings. Trim to cover the beaded piece just below the top picot bead, shown as the blue line in figure 6.

5 Whipstitch the outer-backing to the piece, stitching through the top picot bead (figure 7).

figure 7

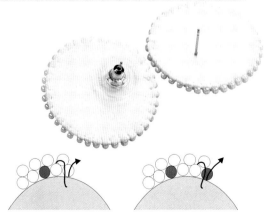

figure 1

figure 2

figure 3

figure 4

figure 5

Midnight Dew Post Earrings

Based on Whole Lotta Luv Post Earrings (page 110)

Key Elements: Paua shell round coin beads, dyed turquoise, 15 mm; fire-polished beads, black opaque, 3 mm; 6-inch (15.2 cm) strand of small cupolini coral beads, turquoise blue; glass faceted rondelle beads, black opaque, 3 x 6 mm; glass faceted teardrops, top and side drilled, 12 x 9 mm

Stitches/Techniques: Standard/Plain Bezel; Clean Edge, switch to Sunshine Edge for 15 beads, then finish with Clean Edge (see lesson below); Fringe Edge—Standard Fringe

lesson

Using Clean Edge with Fringe

The Clean Edge is very useful but does not work well with fringe. Switch from the Clean Edge stitch to the Sunshine Edge stitch to accommodate the fringe work.

• You can decide how many fringes you want. In that case, start with the Clean Edge stitch and stitch five beads. Switch to the Sunshine Edge stitch and use that stitch for as many beads as you want fringes, then switch back to the Clean Edge to complete the edge row.

• You can decide you want the fringe to cover a selected edge area. In that case, start approximately ½ inch (1.3 cm) from the beginning of that area using the Clean Edge. Switch to the Sunshine Edge for the selected area, then switch back to the Clean Edge to complete the edge row.

• You can decide as you bead. In that case, start with the Clean Edge and stitch five or six beads. Switch to the Sunshine Edge and use that stitch for as many beads fringes as desired. Switch back to the Clean Edge and finish the edge row.

If you want a V-shaped fringe, use an odd number of Sunshine Edge row beads.

Add two more Sunshine Edge row beads than your plan. This allows you to easily change your mind and adjust your design.

For the fringe: Start the fringe at the center bottom, at the eighth Sunshine Edge bead. Add the fringes to one side and then the other. There are two different end sequences, each using 11° turquoise beads for the count. End sequence B is one 3 mm, three sets of one black 11° and one cupolini, one black 11°, one faceted rondelle, one 3 mm, and a turn bead using one black 11°. End sequence A is the same except it eliminates the turn bead and adds a drop of four 11° turquoise beads, one teardrop, and four 11° turquoise beads. Stitch through the drop beads again to create a loop and then return up the fringe strand.

Position	Count	End Sequence
Center	17	A
7, 9	14	B
6, 10	12	A
5, 11	10	B
4, 12	8	A
3, 13	6	B
2, 14	4	A
1, 15, not used		

Fringed Drop Wire Earrings

What You Need

2 freshwater pearl coin beads, lime green, 12 mm

26 fire-polished beads, aqua opal, 3 mm

26 fire-polished beads, lime transparent, 4 mm

26 freshwater pearl beads, lime, 5 mm

1 pair of gold ear wires

2 pieces each of backing and outer-backing, 1¼ x 1¼ inches (3.2 x 3.2 cm)

Standard Beading Kit (page 14)

Pliers

Seed Beads

    1 gram of 15° light gold metallic

    1 gram of 11° teal opaque luster

    3 grams of 11° lime color-lined aqua

    1 gram of 8° lime transparent rainbow

    1 gram of twisted bugle beads, aqua transparent rainbow, 12 mm

What You Do

1 Glue the coin pearl bead onto the backing and let it dry. Sew it on with the One-Bead Stitch. Create a Standard/Plain Bezel using the 8° beads for the base row and the 15° beads for the bezel row. Create an additional row with the 11° teal beads.

2 Trim the backing. Apply the outer-backing and trim. Stitch the edge using the Sunshine Edge stitch with the 11° lime beads.

> **tip** Earrings are much easier to execute when the count of the Sunshine Edge row beads is the same for each earring. After trimming, hold the earrings up to each other, back to back, and check that the backings are the same size. Consider trimming one if needed and possible without cutting threads. Create the edge on the smaller one first and count the number of beads used. As you bead the second one, check the count halfway through and adjust the spacing as needed. Do the smaller one first because it is easier and looks better to space out the edge row count than to try and squeeze another bead on an edge, which can create a ripple.

3 Select an edge bead to be the center bottom and start there. Add the fringes to one side and then the other. The fringe is a count of the 11° lime beads with an end sequence of one 11° teal, one bugle bead, one 11° teal, one 3 mm, one 11° teal, one 4 mm, one 11° lime, one 5 mm, and one 15° for the turn bead. Start with a count of 15 and reduce by two for each subsequent fringe. here are a total of 13 fringes (figure 1).

figure 1

> **tip** Use bugle beads to limit the weight of fringe while still adding visual interest.

> **tip** When beading fringe, cut 6 yards (5.5 m) of thread. Take half of the thread and wrap it in a sticky note. Start in the center and use half of the thread for the center fringe and the fringes to the left. Take the sticky note off and use that thread to add fringes to the right. This is the *half-thread method*.

4 Count the Sunshine Edge row beads on each side of the fringe and identify the center top. Create a loop there using six or seven 11° lime beads, based on the lesson Loops on Sunshine Edge on page 107.

5 Stitch the Pointed Edge stitch on the remaining Sunshine Edge row using the 11° lime beads with a 15° bead at the top of the point.

6 Use pliers to open the loop on the ear wire, insert the bead loop, and close the ear wire loop.

7 Repeat steps 1 through 6 for the second earring.

Classic Elegance
Wire Earrings

What You Need

2 metal puffed teardrop beads, brushed gold, 16 x 12 mm

34 glass pearl beads, gold, 3 mm

2 lampwork glass leaf drops, gold, 28 x 12 mm

1 pair of gold ear wires

2 pieces each of backing and outer-backing, 1¼ x 1¼ inches (3.2 x 3.2 cm)

Standard Beading Kit (page 14)

Pliers

Seed Beads:

   1 gram of 15° light gold metallic

   2 grams of 11° light gold metallic

What You Do

1 Glue the teardrop bead onto the backing and let it dry. Sew it on with the One-Bead Stitch.

2 Create a Standard/Plain Bezel using seventeen 3-mm beads and the Couch Stitch for the base row. Use the 15° gold beads for the bezel row. Trim the backing. Apply the outer-backing and trim. Stitch a Clean Edge row using the 11° beads.

3 Find and mark the center top and bottom.

4 See the lesson: Loops on Clean Edge (page 108). Create a loop at the center top using ten 15° beads spaced three or four beads apart. Create a loop at the center bottom using seven 15° beads, the leaf drop, and seven 15° beads for the loop spaced three or four beads apart (figure 1).

figure 1

5 Use pliers to open the loop on the ear wire, insert the bead loop, and close the ear wire loop.

6 Repeat steps 1 through 5 for the second earring.

tip Manage your base row Couch Stitch. Sew one bead on the bottom (figure 2). Lay the beads around the rest of the edge and count the added beads. If the count is even, stitch two beads at the center top (figure 3); if the count is odd, stitch one bead at the center top. Now fill each side with the same count (figure 4).

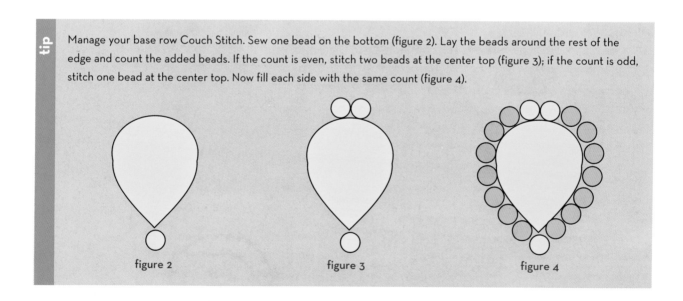

figure 2

figure 3

figure 4

Leaf Love Post Earrings

Based on Classic Elegance Wire Earrings (page 115)

Key Elements: Rhodonite puffed flat oval beads, 16 x 12 mm; hematite leaves, top and side drilled, 23 x 12 mm

Stitches/Techniques: Standard/Plain Bezel, Clean Edge, Using Flashing with Findings Lesson (page 109), Loops on Clean Edge Lesson (page 108)

Chocolate Tiger Wire Earrings

Based on Classic Elegance Wire Earrings (page 115)

Key Elements: Tigereye round cabochons, 8 mm; hollow blown-glass beads, brown, 20 x 35 mm; metal bead caps, bronze, 6 mm

Stitches/Techniques: Standard/Plain Bezel; Sunshine Edge—Picot Variation; Loops on Sunshine Edge—Picot Variation Lesson (page 107)

tip Add pizazz to your designs with choices of dramatically different things. This can be accomplished by choosing colors that are complementary (opposite each other on the color wheel, such as red and green, or black and white) or, as in this project, the size of the components. The cabochon is very small and is combined with a very large bead. The bead is hollow glass, so the issue of weight is successfully addressed.

Sunset Wire Earrings

What You Need

2 rivolis, volcano, 12 mm

2 goldstone rondelle beads, 8 x 4 mm

2 goldstone faceted round beads, 8 mm

14 crystal bicone beads, astral pink, 3 mm

1 pair of gold ear wires

2 pieces each of backing and outer-backing, 1¼ x 1¼ inches (3.2 x 3.2 cm)

2 pieces each of backing and outer-backing, ¾ x ¾ inch (1.9 x 1.9 cm)

Standard Beading Kit (page 14)

Pliers

Seed Beads

    2 grams of 15° dark copper metallic

    4 grams of 11° green color-lined rust

    2 grams of 6° dark copper silk

What You Do

1 Read the lesson: Create a Flat Base (below, right) and create a flat base for the rivoli. The bezel technique used here positions the base row slightly under the rivoli edge, so create a small flat base in the center, not all the way to the edge. Center it on the backing, glue it down, and let it dry. Create a Standard/Plain Bezel using the 6° beads for the base row and the 15° beads for the bezel row. Stitch an additional row using the 11° beads. Trim the backing. Apply the outer-backing and trim it. Stitch the edge with the 11° beads. Start with the Clean Edge stitch for five beads, switch to the Sunshine Edge for four beads, and then resume with the Clean Edge to finish.

2 Glue the rondelle bead onto the backing and let it dry. Stitch on with the Stacks Stitch using the bicone and 15° beads (figures 1 and 2). Create a Standard/Plain Bezel using the 11° beads for the base row and the 15° beads for the bezel row. Trim the backing. Apply the outer-backing and trim it. Stitch the edge using the 11° beads and the Sunshine Edge stitch. Find and mark the center top and bottom.

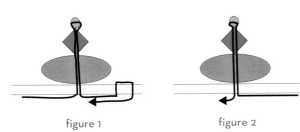

figure 1   figure 2

3 Use the rivoli component and Combine with the rondelle component. Use the center two Sunshine Edge beads on the rivoli component and two edge beads on the rondelle component.

tip Earrings are perfect for using component beading techniques. Add as many components as you like, stop adding, and/or change your mind and rearrange your components as you bead for maximum design possibilities.

4 Identify the center top of the rivoli component. Read the lesson: Loops on Clean Edge (page 108) and add a loop at the center top using eight 15° beads.

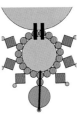

figure 3

5 Finish the edge on the rondelle component using the bicone, 15°, 11°, and 8-mm beads with the fringe stitch as illustrated in figures 3 and 4.

6 Use pliers to open the loop on the ear wire, insert the bead loop, and close the ear wire loop.

7 Repeat steps 1 through 6 for the second earring.

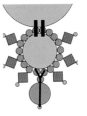

figure 4

Create a Flat Base

Many items selected for use in bead embroidery have an uneven base. This includes shells or metal stampings with a concave underside, round or oval beads that roll, and mineral specimens and rivolis with an uneven surface. Sometimes a focal may slant in one direction and not sit evenly. There are two issues with the bottom surface. One is having enough surface underneath to glue onto the backing. The other is providing an adequate base so the focal doesn't wobble or move when attached and the focal lies as desired. You can create a flat, smooth base using air-dry clay, which is available at most craft stores. Simply use the clay to fill in concave areas, increase the thickness (raise the level), and/or change the angle of how the component sits. Let the clay dry completely. It can be painted a color or sealed with clear nail polish. Glue to the focal and let dry, then glue it to the backing.

Aqua Ice
Post Earrings

What You Need

2 Malaysian jade round cabochons, green, 8 mm

2 agate oval cabochons, teal, 16 x 12 mm

6 aluminum carved teardrop beads, green, 10 x 6 mm

2 glass leaf beads, swirl green and turquoise, 10 x 14 mm

6 fire-polished beads, silver metallic, 3 mm

2 pieces each of backing and outer-backing, 3 x 2 inches (7.6 x 5.1 cm)

2 pieces of flashing, 3 x 2 inches (7.6 x 5.1 cm)

2 ear-post findings

Standard Beading Kit (page 14)

Seed Beads

    1 gram of 15° silver metallic

    1 gram of 15° light aqua ceylon

    1 gram of 11° turquoise opaque luster

    3 grams of 11° light aqua transparent

    1 gram of 6° turquoise opaque

What You Do

1 Draw a vertical center line on the backing. Center the 8-mm round cabochon ½ inch (1.3 cm) from the top edge, glue it on, and let it dry. Create a Standard/Plain Bezel using the 11° aqua beads for the base row and the 15° silver beads for the bezel row. Center the oval cabochon so that it touches the base row, glue it down, and let it dry (figure 1).

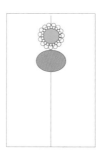

figure 1

2 Create a Standard/Plain Bezel using the 11° turquoise beads for the base row and the 15° aqua beads for the bezel row.

3 Add a row of Backstitch around the round cabochon using the 11° aqua beads. Add a row of Backstitch around the oval cabochon using the 11° turquoise beads. Glue the teardrop beads below the oval cabochon rows and let them dry. Sew each of them on with the One-Bead Stitch (figure 2).

figure 2

4 Stitch a row of Backstitch around the teardrop section using the 11° aqua beads. Use the Stacks Stitch next to the teardrop beads with the 6° beads and a 15° silver bead for the turn bead. Stitch a row of Backstitch around the stack with the 11° aqua beads (figure 3).

figure 3

5 Glue the leaf under the teardrop section row and let it dry. Sew it on with the One-Bead Stitch. Add a row of Backstitch around the leaf using the 11° aqua beads. Fill in around the teardrops with the 11° and 15° aqua beads and One-Bead Stitch.

6 To hide the hole on the bottom of the teardrop bead: Stitch up from the back side at the top of one of the teardrop beads, through the bead, and pick up one 3-mm bead and one 15° silver bead as a turn bead. Stitch back through the 3 mm, the teardrop, and the backing. Repeat for each teardrop (figure 4).

figure 4

> **tip** Stitch large beads on with the One-Bead Stitch. Sometimes the holes are elevated above the surrounding beadwork and look unattractive. As a final step, add a stack through the bead to hide the holes, as in step 6.

7 Trim the backing. Read the lesson Using Flashing with Findings (page 109). Prepare the post according to the lesson, glue it onto the backing, and let it dry.

> **tip** It is not always necessary to add stabilizer to the entire back. Just make sure you cover enough area to provide an adequate gluing surface.

8 Apply the outer-backing and trim it. Use the 11° aqua beads and stitch the edge with the Clean Edge stitch.

> **tip** Use a sewing-machine needle to create a hole in the outer-backing to accommodate the post. The needle has a sharp point and flairs to a large top, which will make a good-size hole.

9 Repeat steps 1 through 8 for the second earring.

CHAPTER 8

Pins

Pins are a versatile jewelry item. Wear them on collars and jacket lapels as well as other wardrobe items such as purses or overcoats.

You use the same design and bead-embroidery techniques for pins that you use for necklaces, earrings, and bracelets; the only difference is the use of a pin finding. This project includes the key construction methods you need to add a pin finding, so you can design any pin you desire.

Blue Danube Pin

What You Need

1 glass cabochon by Linda Sharpsteen, 25 x 22 mm

1 blue agate oval cabochon, 16 x 12 mm

3 glass round beads, bronze metallic, 6 mm

7 glass round beads, bronze metallic, 4 mm

9 fire-polished beads, bronze metallic, 3 mm

1 piece each of backing and outer-backing, 3 x 3½ inches (7.6 x 8.9 cm)

1 piece of flashing, 3 x 3 inches (7.6 x 7.6 cm)

1 pin back, 1¼ inches (3.2 cm)

Standard Beading Kit (page 14)

Seed Beads

  2 grams of 15° bronze metallic

  2 grams of 15° blue metallic matte

  2 grams of 11° blue opaque

  2 grams of 11° navy blue matte

  2 grams of 11° bronze metallic

  2 grams of 11° turquoise blue color-lined

  2 grams of 8° bronze metallic

  2 grams of 8° medium blue matte

  2 grams of 6° turquoise opaque matte

  2 grams of 6° bronze metallic

  2 grams of 6° dark blue matte

What You Do

1 Draw a vertical center line on the backing. Center the glass cabochon on the line ¾ inch (1.9 cm) from the top, glue it down, and let it dry. Create a Standard/Plain Bezel using the turquoise and bronze 6° beads for the base row and the blue and bronze 15° beads for the bezel row. Start at 12 o'clock with the turquoise beads. Switch to the bronze at 3 o'clock and go back to the turquoise at 6 o'clock. Match the bezel colors to the base colors.

2 Read the lesson Curves, Bugles, and the Lazy Stitch (page 125). Stitch a curve of Lazy Stitch using the bugle beads and 11° beads for the straight column and the bronze 8°, 11°, and 15° beads for the triangle columns. Stitch the curve from 3 o'clock to 6 o'clock, matching the bronze beads on the base row. Glue on the agate cabochon, touching the Lazy Stitch row as illustrated in figure 1, and let it dry.

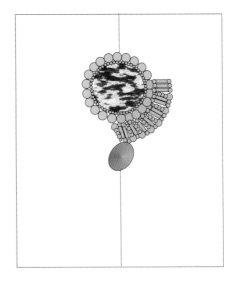

figure 1

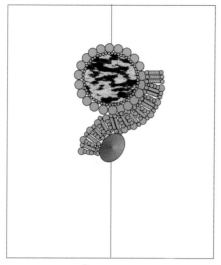

figure 2

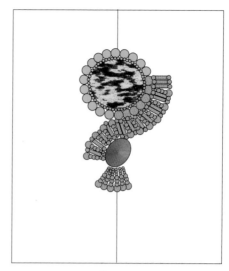

figure 3

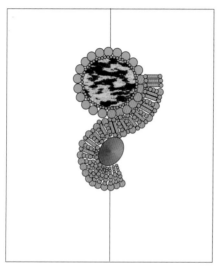

figure 4

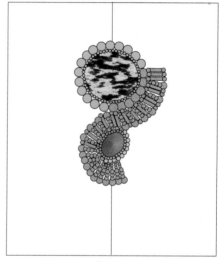

figure 5

3 Continue stitching the curve of Lazy Stitch around the agate cabochon, extending the curve around the bottom cabochon and stopping halfway (figure 2). Start a new section on the bottom, using only the triangle column of the Lazy Stitch (figure 3). Finally, join the sections with beads used in the triangle as needed to fill (figure 4). Complete the base row around the agate cabochon with the 11° blue beads. Create a bezel row using the 15° beads, changing from bronze to blue with the color change in the base row (figure 5).

4 Stitch a row of Backstitch around the top cabochon using the 8° blue beads. Stitch another row of Backstitch using the 11° blue opaque beads. Use the Stacks Stitch with the 6° blue beads and an 11° bronze bead for the turn bead and stitch around the Backstitch rows. The last added row should line up with the edge of the Lazy Stitch. If not, add another row of Backstitch using the 11° navy beads.

5 Use the Stacks Stitch with the 6° blue beads and an 11° bronze bead for the turn bead and stitch around the agate cabochon from the curve up. Stitch a row of Backstitch using the 11° turquoise beads. Stitch another Backstitch row using the 11° blue opaque beads. Stitch another Backstitch row using the 11° navy beads. The last added row should line up with the edge of the Lazy Stitch. If not, add another row of Backstitch using the 11° navy beads.

6 Stitch one more row around the top cabochon and the bottom cabochon. Use the 11° navy and bronze beads and change colors to match the previous rows. Trim the backing.

7 Read the lesson Using Flashing with Findings (page 109) and glue the flashing with the attached pin back onto the backing. Apply the outer-backing and trim it.

> **tip**
>
> When you trim the backing, if the border is in one piece, you can lay that over the flashing to determine the trim line for the flashing.

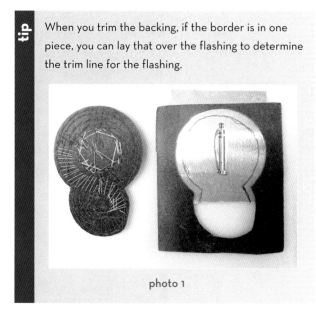

photo 1

> **tip**
>
> Pin backs can be positioned horizontally, vertically, or on any angle you choose. Consider positioning the pin finding so that a chain can be strung through it and the piece can be worn as a pendant necklace for maximum wearability. See photo 1 for the positioning used on this project.

8 Stitch the edge with the 11° navy and bronze beads using the Sunshine Edge. Change colors based on the previous beadwork.

9 Add fringes using the 6-mm, 4-mm, 3-mm, 11°, and 15° bronze beads. Adjust your fringe design as needed to position it at the center bottom (figure 6).

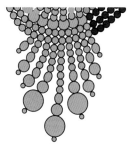

figure 6

10 Use the 15° bronze beads with the Pointed Edge Stitch to finish the edge beads that are bronze colored.

Curves, Bugles, and the Lazy Stitch

Curves and Lazy Stitch are tricky. The Lazy Stitch—whether it is all seed beads or includes a bugle bead—is a column. If applied to a curve and beaded sideways to the curve (figure 7), it provides an interesting effect and covers the backing appropriately. However, if it is applied around a curve (figure 8), there will be gaps between the columns and the backing will show. If you choose to do that method, be sure to choose a backing that is attractive when seen.

figure 7

figure 8

Below are two methods to bead around a curve but not show the backing:

The first method (used in the Ruby Curve Necklace, page 33, as well as the Blue Danube Pin) is to include a Lazy Stitch column that is shaped like a triangle. You can accomplish this by using 15°, 11°, 8°, and even 6° beads to construct that column. Select the beads, both size and counts, for the triangle based on the length of the regular Lazy Stitch column. Use radiating lines to assist in determining when to stitch a triangle Lazy Stitch versus the regular columns. When the regular columns slant in a different direction than the radiating lines, add a triangle column (figure 9).

figure 9

The second method is to layer the columns. First stitch around the curve, spacing the stitches to leave a gap one bead wide between the columns on the outside of the stitch (figure 10). Bead around the curve again with Lazy Stitch on top of the stitches already placed there to cover the gaps. Figure 11 shows this with two colors for illustration purposes only; you can stitch the second row with the same color as the first. The second row sits on top of the first row on the inside of the curve.

figure 10   figure 11

CHAPTER 9

Bracelets

Bracelets are popular jewelry items to make with bead embroidery techniques, second only to necklaces. The information that follows covers design and construction issues that are unique to bracelets.

Findings

Each project in this chapter includes instructions to create a beaded loop and to use jump rings for attaching the bracelet clasp. Constructing bracelets this way is useful for several reasons:

• There is more stress and knocking on a bracelet clasp than any other finding, so the chance of the clasp breaking is greater. When the clasp is attached with jump rings, any breakage or other problem with the clasp is easily solved by just opening the jump rings and attaching a new clasp.

• Many people have strong opinions and preferences for either silver or gold for their jewelry. This is especially true with bracelets because they want the findings to match their watch or other jewelry. If the clasp is attached with jump rings, it's easy to switch from gold to silver, or vice versa.

• Bracelets need to be different lengths to fit different people—not all wrists are the same size. You can easily resize a bracelet when the clasp is attached with

jump rings: you simply change the style or type of clasp to make it smaller or larger. You can add more jump rings or beads between the loop and the clasp to make it longer. Even ¼ inch (6 mm) is a significant size change in a bracelet, so this is an important design point to consider.

Edges

Do *not* use the raw Sunshine Edge for your edge treatment for two reasons. First, this edge has exposed thread. Any time thread is exposed it creates the potential for breaking and/or getting soiled. Bracelets are worn on a part of the body with active movement, which creates more potential for wear and breakage. Second, it is just not attractive. Bracelet edges are exposed in a way that necklace edges aren't, so the choice of the edge treatment is more important. The projects that follow include numerous ways to design and create edges on bracelets.

Bracelet Forms Page

A useful tool for necklace design is the Neck Form Page (page 12), and there is an equivalent for bracelets. First, recognize that not all bracelets should fit the same. A wide bracelet and a cuff bracelet are typically worn tighter and higher on the wrist than other bracelet styles. So, having more than one form on your page is useful. You use the same method to make a Bracelet Forms Page as you do for the Neck Form Page, so first, go and get some string.

1 Drape the string around your wrist in the area where you want a bead-strand style of bracelet to hang. This will typically be approximately 1 inch (2.5 cm) down from your wrist, but it's also a matter of personal preference. Cut the string and measure it with a ruler. Draw that length on a piece of paper (the Bracelet Forms Page), starting the line at the leftmost side of the page. Label the line with the word *draped*. Use a ruler and mark the center with a small vertical line.

2 Take the same string and form it into a circle on the page below the line. Draw that circle. Write *draped* inside the circle. Draw a line down the middle of the circle.

3 Use the same string and measure around your wrist where you would wear a watch. Insert one finger under the string, increasing the length a bit to add ease for comfort. Cut the string and measure it with a ruler. Draw that length on the Bracelet Forms Page below the circle created in step 2. Label the line *cuff*. Use a ruler and mark the center with a small vertical line.

4 Finally, set your wrist down on the paper, centered and below the line drawn in step 3. Draw a short line on each side that will mark the width of your wrist. Lift your wrist up and connect the two lines with a ruler. Label the line *width*.

This is the *Bracelet Forms Page*. Use the lines to measure your beadwork as you create. Be sure to consider the lengths needed on each end to accommodate the bead loops, jump rings, and clasp. You can roll the page up into a tube connecting the ends of either the draped line or the cuff line (figure 1). Secure it with paper clips and use it to test the fit in three dimensions.

figure 1

The "width" is a measurement of the front of the bracelet. One inch (2.5 cm) on each side will be worn on the sides of the wrist, and the remainder is the back of the wrist. This is critical to understand in order to design a comfortable, wearable bracelet. The width is the prime design area, the portion that will be most visible. You can safely use large, chunky, and tall beadwork in that area. However, using those same beads and techniques on the sides or back can make the bracelet uncomfortable to wear, and tall focals on the sides will stick out and may not look good.

Watch Me
Bracelet

What You Need

1 dichroic glass square cabochon, 20 x 20 mm

48 to 56 crystal bicone beads, aquamarine, 3 mm

24 to 32 fire-polished beads, red carmen, 6 mm

8 to 12 crystal bicone beads, aquamarine, 4 mm

1 piece each of backing and outer-backing, 1¾ x 1¾ inches (4.4 x 4.4 cm)

Two 9-inch (22.9 cm) lengths of .019-diameter flexible beading wire

4 gold crimp beads

1 gold two-hole slide clasp

8 gold jump rings, 5 mm

Standard Beading Kit (page 14)

Crimping pliers

Wire cutters

Pliers

Seed Beads

    1 gram of 15° turquoise transparent rainbow

    3 grams of 11° garnet AB

    2 grams of 6° turquoise transparent rainbow

What You Do

1 Glue the cabochon onto the backing and let it dry. Create a Standard/Plain Bezel using the 6° beads for the base row and the 15° beads for the bezel row. Stitch an additional row using the 11° beads.

> **tip**
>
> Glass melts to a standard thickness. Although some glass artists manipulate the edges, the other fused-glass cabochons have the same edge thickness. A 6° bead for the base row works perfectly for lifting the bezel row to the area where the cabochon slopes and will properly secure the cabochon.

2 Trim the backing. Apply the outer-backing and trim. Use the 11° beads to stitch the edge with the Sunshine Edge stitch. Stitch the edge with the Rope Edge— Middle Bead Variation using the 11° and 3-mm beads.

3 Position a needle from the front through the backings to the back side between the base row and the additional row at each corner (figures 1 and 2). Use a marker and put a small dot on the back where the needle is sticking out. Cull the 11° beads and select four with large holes; stitch one on each of the marked spots, positioning the holes as illustrated in figure 3 using the Back Side Bead Attachment method.

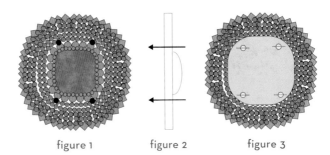

figure 1   figure 2   figure 3

4 Place the beaded component on the Bracelet Forms Page (page 127), centered on the line you want for the bracelet fit (typically the Cuff Line because this is a wide bracelet design). Turn it upside down so the back shows. String one of the beading wires through one of the back-side beads. Pick up the 11° beads to span the distance to the back-side bead on the other side (figure 4).

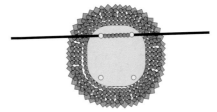

figure 4

5 String the 11° beads onto the wire to span the distance across the edge. Use the 6-mm, 4-mm, and 11° beads and string on the bracelet portion. Stop ¾ inch (1.9 cm) before the end of the line measurement on your Bracelet Forms Page. Pick up one 6°, one crimp bead, and nine 11° beads. String the end back through the crimp bead and 6° beads (figure 5). Crimp and trim. Repeat on the other side.

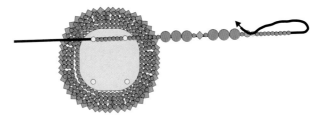

figure 5

6 Use the other beading wire strand and repeat steps 4 and 5 with the other back-side beads.

7 Use the pliers and jump rings to attach the clasp.

> **tip**
>
> If you have components left over because of design changes when creating a necklace, this design is a great way to use them. Use the Rope Edge to make the component much larger. Use one of the other edge techniques if you don't need a size adjustment.

Midnight Dreams Bracelet

Based on Watch Me Bracelet (page *128*)

Key Elements: Montana agate polished slice rectangle, 25 x 20 mm; fire-polished beads, black, 3 mm; glass faceted round disk beads, black opaque, 10 mm and 8 mm

Stitches/Techniques: Bugle Row Bezel, Picot Stitch, Couch Stitch, Clean Edge on the top and bottom using 3-mm beads, Sunshine Edge on the sides, Side Petal Edge, Standard Necklace Instructions for Direct Attachment Sunshine Edge—Single Edge Bead (page 145)

> **tip**
> Tip: You can use contrasting thread with the Picot Stitch for interesting design effects.

> **tip**
> Typically the Clean Edge is used with 11° beads; however, you can use other beads such as 3-mm fire-polished beads, 8° hex beads, and many others for interesting design effects.

Sea World Bracelet

Based on Watch Me Bracelet (page *128*)

Key Elements: Lampwork glass puffed round bead, 24 mm; picture jasper rondelle beads, 12 mm; glass stone-effect round beads, tan, 6 mm; glass stone-effect twisted oval beads, tan, 8 x 15 mm; crystal bicone beads, Caribbean blue opal, 3 mm

Stitches/Techniques: Standard/Plain Bezel, Stacks Stitch, Sunshine Edge, Side Petal Edge, Standard Necklace Instructions for Direct Attachment Sunshine Edge—Single Edge Bead (page 145)

Rich 'n Red Bracelet

What You Need

1 moukaite puffed flat marquis bead, 20 x 40 mm

2 freshwater pearl sticks, long drilled, dyed gold, 25 mm

2 Malaysian jade puffed flat oval beads, dyed red, 18 x 25 mm

4 to 8 moukaite faceted round beads, 6 mm

1 piece each of backing and outer-backing, 2 x 3 inches (5.1 x 7.6 cm)

4 pieces each of backing and outer-backing, 2 x 2½ inches (5.1 x 6.4 cm)

1 gold two-hole slide clasp

8 gold jump rings, 5 mm

Standard Beading Kit (page 14)

Pliers

Seed Beads

    3 grams of 15° cranberry gold luster

    8 grams of 11° dark red transparent

    8 grams of 8° bronze metallic

What You Do

1 Glue the moukaite marquis bead onto the 2 x 3-inch (5.1 x 7.6 cm) piece of backing. Glue the pearl sticks and Malaysian jade beads onto the other pieces of backing. Let all dry.

2 For each focal: Sew the bead on with the One-Bead Stitch. Create a Standard/Plain Bezel using the 8° beads for the base row and the 15° beads for the bezel row. For the moukaite and Malaysian jade components, add an extra row using the 11° beads. Trim the backing. Apply the outer-backing and trim it.

3 The edge is the Clean Edge and has combination areas for three attachment edge beads. Read the lesson Using Clean Edge When Combining (below) and complete the steps. Additionally, stitch five Sunshine Edge beads on the ends of the bracelet to use to create loops for attaching the clasp. Use the 11° beads for the edge.

4 Use the middle three Sunshine Edge beads to Combine the components as illustrated in figure 1.

figure 1

5 Read the lesson Adjusting Size for a Component Bracelet (page 134). Create the end loops with the 6-mm and 11° beads as illustrated in figure 2 or adjust as described in the lesson.

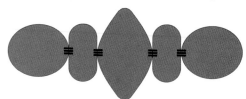

figure 2

6 Use the pliers and jump rings to attach the clasp.

Using Clean Edge When Combining

The Clean Edge is an attractive, useful edge stitch, but it's difficult to use when you want to design with components and attach one component to another. The Sunshine Edge stitch works much better for combining. So, first plan your edge using these steps.

1 Trace each component onto paper. Hold the paper up to a light and fold it, matching the lines so the folds will be in the center (top and bottom or center sides, whichever will be used for the attachment spot). Mark the fold with a marker edge to create a line on the paper.

2 Decide how many edge beads you want to use for attachment stitching (typically two to five). Add two to that number. There is a height difference between the Clean Edge and the Sunshine Edge, so there needs to be a spare Sunshine Edge stitch on each side. For example, if there will be three edge beads used to stitch the attachment, then the calculated number is five (three plus two).

3 Take the beads that will be used for the edge and count out the number of beads calculated in step 2. Lay them edge to edge on the sticky portion of a sticky note so they don't move around (figure 3) and measure the length.

figure 3

4 Place the component back on the traced paper. Identify the area on the edge of the component where you want to attach to another component. Using the measurement from step 3 (and the fold line to help center it), make a small mark on the edge using a pen at the beginning and the end of the measurement area. Do this for each attachment area on each component.

5 Start the edge stitching with the Clean Edge stitch. When you reach a mark showing an attachment area, switch to the Sunshine Edge stitch. Stitch the calculated number, then switch back to the Clean Edge stitch to complete the edge.

Marquis
Magic
Bracelet

What You Need

1 African turquoise puffed flat marquis bead, 28 x 15 mm

4 magnesite puffed flat teardrop beads, 10 x 12 mm

4 tigereye round cabochons, 10 mm

4 tigereye faceted round beads, 8 mm (number of beads is optional for size adjustment)

1 piece each of backing and outer-backing, 2¼ x 1½ inches (5.7 x 3.8 cm)

4 pieces each of backing and outer-backing, 1¼ x 1 inch (3.2 x 2.5 cm)

4 pieces each of backing and outer-backing, 1 x 1 inch (2.5 x 2.5 cm)

1 gold toggle clasp

4 gold jump rings, 5 mm

Standard Beading Kit (page 14)

Pliers

Seed Beads

    2 grams of 15° bronze metallic

    3 grams of 15° root beer transparent matte

    5 grams of 11° root beer transparent

    1 gram of 11° turquoise opaque

    2 grams of 6° root beer transparent

What You Do

1 Match up the African turquoise bead, magnesite beads, and tigereye cabochons with the appropriate size of backing pieces (largest to largest, etc.). Glue the beads and cabochons onto the backings and let them dry. Sew on the beads with the One-Bead Stitch.

2 Create a Standard/Plain Bezel for the African turquoise component. Use the 6° beads for the base row and the 15° bronze beads for the bezel row. Stitch an additional row using the 11° turquoise beads.

> **tip** The 6° base row uses a light thread with the transparent root beer beads to create a glow effect.

3 For the other components, create a Standard/Plain Bezel using the 11° root beer beads for the base row and the 15° bronze beads for the bezel row.

4 For each component: Trim the backing. Apply the outer-backing and trim. Stitch the edge using the 11° root beer beads and the Sunshine Edge stitch. Find and mark the center top and bottom.

> **tip** Mark the center top and bottom of the components when doing pieced component construction. Even if the center top and bottom are not used for a connection point, they still provide a valuable reference. For

example, if the connection is four beads down from the center top on one side, then it is easy to duplicate on the other side using the same count.

5 On a piece of paper, draw horizontal and vertical center lines. Lay the components on the paper, arranged as in figure 1. Construction for a pieced bracelet is just like that for a pieced necklace. Read the lesson Combining Multiple Components (page 77). Combine the components as described.

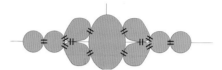

figure 1

6 Lay the piece on your Bracelet Forms Page—Cuff Line to test the size. Read the lesson Adjusting Size for a Component Bracelet below. Create the end loops with the 8-mm and 11° beads as illustrated in figure 2, or adjust them per the lesson.

figure 2

7 Complete the edge using the Turn Bead Edge stitch with the 15° root beer beads.

> **tip** The Turn Bead Edge using a 15° bead creates a smooth line and a very small increase in the size of the bracelet. It hides the holes of the Sunshine Edge and protects and hides the thread. This is a perfect edge technique to fix the edge appearance on bracelets you've previously created.

> **lesson**
> ## Adjusting Size for a Component Bracelet
>
> There are several options for finishing the bracelet to make it fit a desired size.
>
> • If the size is as desired, simply create loops at the end and use a small clasp such as a slide clasp.
>
> • If you want a larger, longer bracelet, you can add a component on each end using the same beads, bezels, and edges as the previous components. Select a focal bead or cabochon size 8 mm or larger, depending on how much length you want to add.
>
> • You can make the bracelet slightly longer by adding one or more beads into the loop creation.
>
> • Use a larger clasp or add a series of jump rings when attaching the clasp.

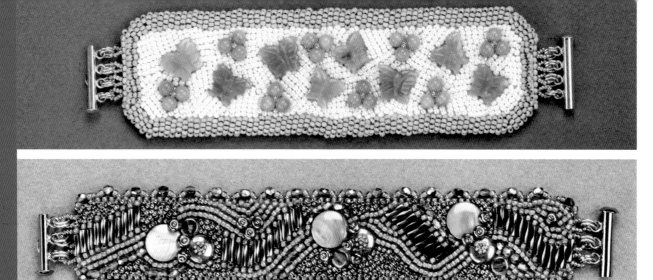

CHAPTER 10

Cuffs

Cuff bracelets have a unique attribute. The previous projects had flexibility and hinging action within the designs. Cuff designs, however, bend throughout the beaded area of the bracelet. This bending can open up spaces between the beads and expose the backing material the beads are sewn on.

There are three ways to address this:

• Select a backing with an acceptable appearance so that when it shows, it looks fine. The Surfing the Wave Bracelet (bottom photo, above) uses Ultrasuede stabilized with iron-on interfacing. The Ultrasuede is an attractive surface, but it needs the interfacing to provide a stable surface to bead on.

• Design around the issue. The exposure is most severe when there are rows of beads that parallel the bent area, but stitching rows on angles there solves this problem. Both of the projects that follow (Surfing the Wave Bracelet, page 136, and Halloween Holiday Bracelet, page 139) are examples of this approach.

• Stitch beads over the exposure areas. Create stacks, or stitch another row on top and midway between rows to hide exposed areas. The beaded collar Magic Forest Necklace (page 69) uses this approach (see step 14, page 72).

Although the projects in this chapter are for soft cuffs, you can easily adapt the designs to hard cuffs by shortening, lengthening, and/or widening the designs to fit a purchased hard cuff form.

These are the steps for creating hard cuffs:

1 Select a hard cuff form.

2 Create a pattern using paper based on the cuff surface that is at least ¼ inch (6 mm) wider on all sides. Cut out the pattern; test it on the cuff form. Adjust as necessary.

3 Trace the pattern onto the backing. Trim and bead the backing as desired.

4 Apply glue to the outside of the cuff form and attach the beadwork. Start at one end, and wrap to the other end.

5 Trace the pattern created in step 2 onto the outer-backing. Cut it out on the lines.

6 Apply glue to the inside of the cuff form. Start at one end and apply the outer-backing, matching it to the edge of the beaded backing already attached. Wrap around the inside to the other end. Trim the other end to match the beaded backing size. Although these pieces were created with the same pattern, one is wrapped outside the cuff and the other inside, so they end up different lengths because of the curve.

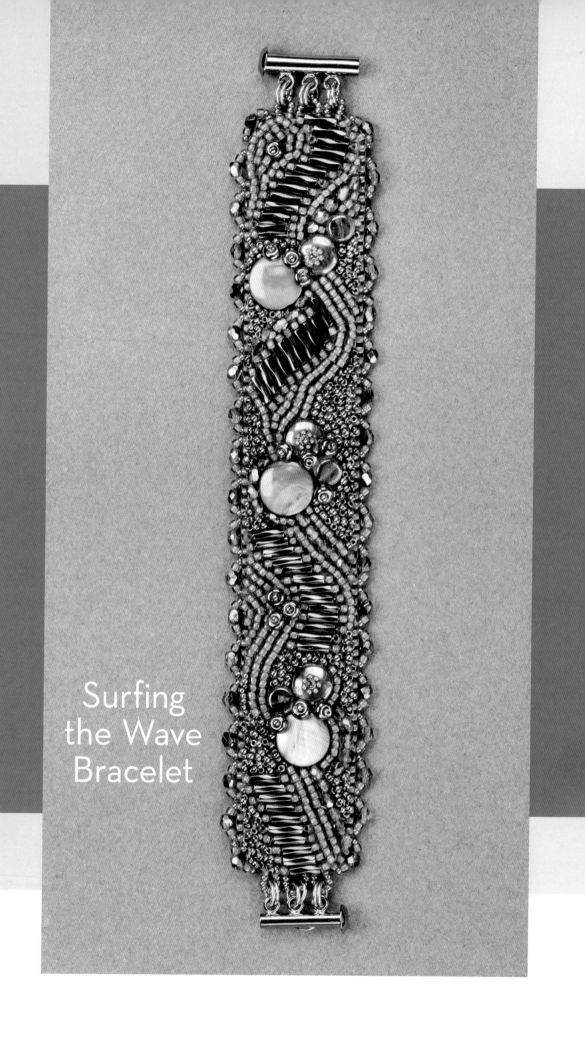

Surfing
the Wave
Bracelet

What You Need

3 mother-of-pearl flat round beads, dyed purple, 12 mm

3 glass rondelle beads, green AB, 8 mm

3 glass coin beads, purple AB, 6 mm

3 metal rondelles, antique gold, 4 mm

59 to 72 fire-polished beads, green and purple two-tone, 3 mm

2 pieces each of Ultrasuede, 7 x 1½ inches (17.8 x 3.8 cm)

1 piece of lightweight iron-on interfacing, 7 x 1½ inches (17.8 x 3.8 cm)

1 three-hole slide clasp

12 jump rings, 5 mm

Standard Beading Kit (page 14)

Pliers

Seed Beads

> 3 grams of 15° green metallic AB
>
> 10 grams of 11° purple color-lined
>
> 1 gram of 6° green metallic AB
>
> 2 grams of bugle beads, purple metallic AB, 6 mm

What You Do

1 Fuse the iron-on interfacing to one piece of the Ultrasuede following the manufacturer's instructions. In the center of the backing, draw a rectangle that is 6 x ⅞ inches (15.2 x 2.2 cm) (figure 1). Cut on the lines. Trim the corners diagonally approximately ⅛ inch (3 mm) (figure 2).

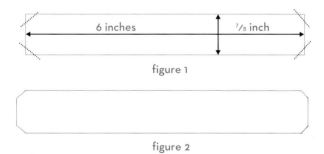

figure 1

figure 2

2 Draw lines on the backing as illustrated in figure 3.

figure 3

3 Stitch on beads with the Lazy Stitch using one 11°, one bugle, and one 11°. Stitch using the angles as illustrated just above the line so that the first 11° bead will lie over the drawn lines (figure 4).

figure 4

4 Glue on the 12-mm, 8-mm, and 6-mm beads as illustrated in figure 5. Let them dry. Sew on the 12-mm and 6-mm beads using the One-Bead Stitch. Use the Stacks Stitch with the 8-mm bead, adding one 4-mm rondelle and one 11° as the turn bead.

figure 5

5 Refer to figure 6 for this step. Start on the right side of the bracelet. In the center area above the bugles, stitch a stack using a 6° bead and an 11° as the turn bead as illustrated in green. Create a row of Backstitch using the 11° beads around the edge as indicated in orange and fill with rows of Backstitch. Stitch a row of Backstitch using the 11° beads under the bugle strip as indicated in orange. Follow that line and stitch a row of Backstitch using the 3-mm fire-polished beads. Fill the area below with Backstitch using the 11° beads. Fill the area above with Picot Stitch using the 15° beads.

figure 6

6 Refer to figure 7 for this step. Create a row of Backstitch using the 11° beads from the center cluster to the right cluster as indicated in orange. Create two more rows under that. Create a row of Backstitch using the 3-mm fire-polished beads on the edge of the bugle strip. Fill the area to the right with Picot Stitch using the 15° beads. Fill the area below with Picot Stitch using the 15° beads.

figure 7

7 Refer to figure 8 for this step. Create a row of Backstitch using 11° beads from the top of the bugle strip to the center of the middle cluster. Continue the row on top of the cluster and over to the next bugle strip as indicated in orange in figure 8. Use the 3-mm fire-polished beads with the Backstitch to create a row below the bugle strip, then make another row of Backstitch using the 11° beads. Fill the area below with Picot Stitch using the 15° beads. Fill the area above and to the right with Backstitch rows using the 11° beads. Add a row of Backstitch using the 3-mm fire-polished beads above the cluster. Add a row of Backstitch using the 11° beads above that. Fill the area remaining to the right and left above with Picot Stitch using the 15° beads.

figure 8

8 Refer to figure 9 for this step. Use the Backstitch and the 11° beads to create a row above the bugle strip and over to the last cluster as illustrated in orange. Fill above with Backstitch using 11° beads. Create a row of Backstitch under the last bugle strip, and two more rows under that with the 11° beads. Create a row of Backstitch from the three rows around the bottom of the cluster using the 11° beads. Create a row of Backstitch to the right of that row using the 3-mm fire-polished beads. Fill the area to the right with Picot Stitch using the 15° beads. Create a row of Backstitch using the 3-mm fire-polished beads below the three rows. Fill the bottom area and all remaining areas with Picot Stitch using 15° beads.

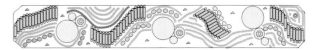

figure 9

9 Use the Stacks Stitch to add texture and cover the gaps between the large beads used in the clusters, positioned as illustrated in pink (figure 10). For the stack, use one 6° and one 11° (turn bead). The top of the stacks should be raised above the beaded surface, so use one to three 15° seed beads in the stack as needed when positioning into a gap.

figure 10

10 Apply the outer-backing and trim. Use the 11° beads and stitch the edge with the Sunshine Edge stitch.

11 Set the clasp near the edge to identify the edge beads to use to create the loops. Read the lesson Loops on a Sunshine Edge, page 107, and create loops on the ends using seven 15° beads (figure 11). Increase the bracelet size by adding a bead into the loop as illustrated (figure 12).

figure 11   figure 12

12 Use the 3-mm, 11°, and 15° beads and stitch the edge with the Side Petal Edge stitch.

13 Use the pliers and jump rings to attach the clasp.

Halloween Holiday Bracelet

What You Need

3 glass flat round pumpkin beads, 12 mm

2 metal spider beads, silver, 15 mm

1 piece each of backing and outer-backing, 1¼ x 8 inches (3.2 x 20.3 cm)

1 three-hole silver slide clasp

12 silver jump rings, 5 mm

Standard Beading Kit (page 14)

Pliers

Seed Beads

    1 gram of 15° black opaque

    1 gram of 15° orange color-lined

    12 grams of 11° orange color-lined

    6 grams of 11° black opaque

    3 grams of 11° gray pearl

What You Do

1 Take the 1¼-inch (3.2 cm) strip of backing and trim it to the length desired. The ends will be finished with beaded loops, jump rings, and a slide clasp, accounting for approximately 1 inch (2.5 cm) of length. Use the cuff measurement of your Bracelet Forms Page (page 127). Cut the strip to that measurement less the 1 inch (2.5 cm) for the clasp area.

2 Draw a vertical center line. Mark ¼ inch (6 mm) inside the edge on the entire piece.

3 Set the focal beads in the interior box and position them in a design you like. (The project spacing is illustrated in figure 2.)

> **tip** Concentrate focal placement and design in the center area using the width measurement on your Bracelet Forms Page as a guide. Alternatively, you can use 2¼ inches (5.7 cm). When laying on a flat surface, there seems to be a boring, empty area on each side of the center decoration. However, when worn, the perspective changes and it looks attractive.

4 Glue the pumpkin beads onto the backing and let them dry. Sew them on with the One-Bead Stitch. The spider bead used has a different profile than most beads, as illustrated in figure 1. The hole sits below the main part of the bead decoration, similar to a shank

on a button. Mark the backing with an oval where the bottom of the spider bead sits.

figure 1

> **tip** Buttons with a short shank are interesting focals to use in bead embroidery. The method used for the spider bead in steps 4 through 6 works great for adding short-shank buttons to surface embroidery.

5 Use the 11° orange beads and fill the inside area with Lazy Stitch. Don't stitch inside the oval area reserved for the spider bead. Start with a stitch of five beads and do four rows. Change direction and repeat (figure 2). Continue until the inside area is covered, adjusting the row and bead count as needed.

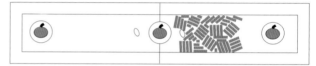

figure 2

6 Fit the spider beads into the blank oval areas and sew them on with the One-Bead Stitch. Stitch a row of Backstitch around the pumpkin beads using the 15° black beads.

7 Review the surface of the beadwork. Use the 11° and 15° orange beads to fill in the gaps of the surface. Apply the outer-backing and trim.

8 Read the lesson Lazy Edge Stitch around a Corner (page 141). Stitch the edge with the 11° black and gray beads. Use the Lazy Edge stitch in a pattern, alternating four black stitches with two gray stitches, except use black only on the ends.

9 Set the clasp near the end and identify the Lazy Edge stitches you will use to create the end loops (figure 3). Stitch through the backing and up through beads in the edge until you get near the top. Pick up beads for the loop and stitch down through the edge beads on the other side and through the backing (figure 4). Repeat the thread path several times to reinforce it. Repeat for each loop and on the other end of the bracelet.

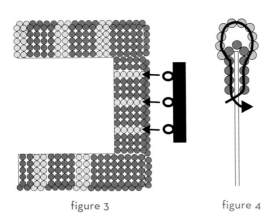

figure 3

figure 4

10 Use the pliers and jump rings to attach the clasp.

Lazy Edge Stitch around a Corner

1 Continue the Lazy Edge stitch to the end.

2 Stitch through the beads of the last few stitches to anchor the placement so the rows don't move (figures 5 and 6).

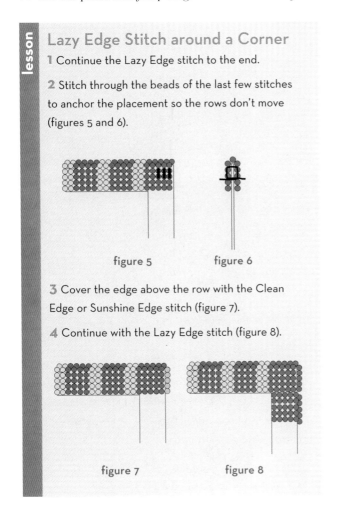

figure 5   figure 6

3 Cover the edge above the row with the Clean Edge or Sunshine Edge stitch (figure 7).

4 Continue with the Lazy Edge stitch (figure 8).

figure 7   figure 8

Summer Solstice Bracelet

Based on Halloween Holiday Bracelet (page 139)

Key Elements: New jade butterfly beads, 12 mm; coral round beads, 5 mm

Stitches/Techniques: One-Bead Stitch, Lazy Stitch, Clover Stitch, Lazy Edge, Lazy Edge Stitch around a Corner Lesson (page 141)

tip You can use the basic instructions for the project, change the beads, and create a bracelet for every holiday—or every day.

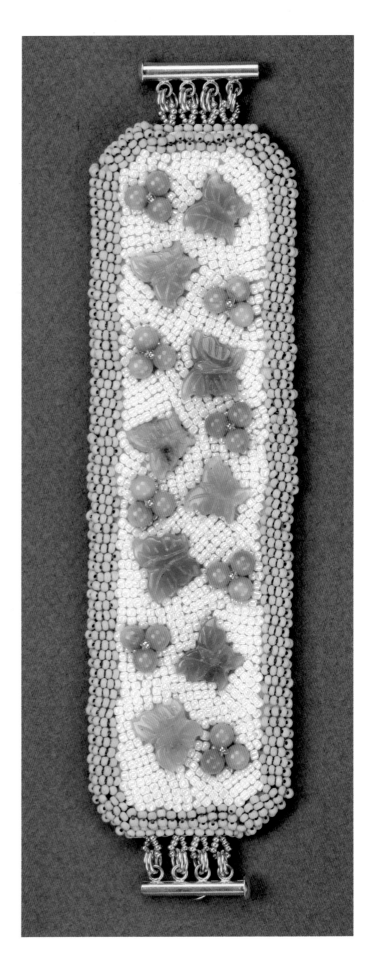

Basic Procedures

Finding and Marking Centers

1 Set the beadwork down on paper and trace around it with a pen (photo 1).

2 Hold the paper up to the light and fold it in half, matching the lines. With a designer-cut or asymmetrical shape you can't match the lines; instead, check to see that the area of one side is roughly equal to the area of the other side. While folded, run the edge of a marker on the fold line (photo 2).

3 Open the paper and place the beadwork on it. Mark the center beads by sticking a needle in them.

4 Count the beads between the top and the bottom when using a symmetrical shape with a Sunshine Edge to test the center marks and adjust as needed. When using the Clean Edge stitch, counting is not necessary. Stitch a piece of thread through the center beads and knot it (photo 3). For asymmetrical shapes, including designer cuts, test the result by holding the thread and let the beadwork dangle to see whether it hangs the way you want. This will test how gravity affects the design. Look at it from the back side. The back is smooth, so it is easier to concentrate on the effect of your selection. Adjust as needed after reviewing how it looks from the front and the back.

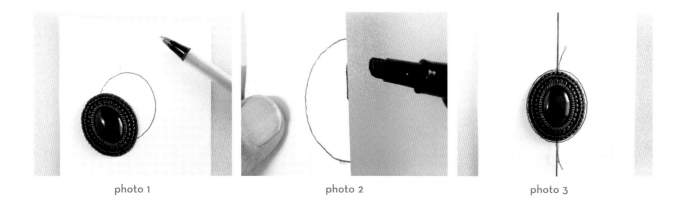

photo 1   photo 2   photo 3

Using Stabilizers

Sometimes it is desirable to increase the stiffness of a piece of bead embroidery. This is accomplished with the use of a stabilizer, which is glued to the backing before the outer-backing is applied. Trim the stabilizer to at least ¼ inch (6 mm) inside the edge of the backing to allow room for edge stitches. Acceptable materials to use for stabilizers include plastic and metal. Plastic report covers (available at office supply stores) are easy to use and can be cut with scissors. Flashing is a thin metal used in roofing; it is available at hardware stores and can be cut with tin snips or heavy-duty scissors. Do not use cardboard; it will cause problems if the beadwork gets wet—if, for example, you get stuck in a rainstorm.

Be cautious when deciding to use a stabilizer because it will make the beadwork very stiff. This is desirable on pins and earrings. Necklaces, however, often need some suppleness to curve around the body. Pendants often can be stabilized without a problem. But collars, bibs, and long totems on a consolidated backing need to have a gentle curve to hang properly and wear comfortably. If you have an area on a collar or bib that you want to stabilize, consider cutting the stabilizer to fit a small area—don't cover the entire backing.

Trimming

Trimming is an essential process used in bead embroidery. Backings are trimmed (cut), and beads are sewn onto the edge, which creates the final profile of the beadwork. If the edge line created by trimming is jagged and wavy, the edge of the final piece will be jagged and wavy.

There are essentially two different methods to use for trimming. One method is to execute the beading, then trim the backing. The trim line in this case is just outside the edge of the surface beadwork. After trimming, there should be just a sliver of backing seen on the edge from the front of the beadwork. The other method is to cut the shape, then fill in with beads. Which method you choose is generally your choice. Although it may be difficult to execute beading up to a cut edge, it can be equally difficult to execute beading within a drawn line. However, if the edge is already cut, you completely eliminate the danger of cutting a thread when trimming. Even if you have superior skills in stitch placement, it is very easy to stray outside a line. When you trim after stitching, your choice is either to cut a thread or compromise on the edge line appearance. The safest method is to precut the edge and avoid potential dangers. Your skill level will increase over time with practice, and stitching to the edge will become easier and easier.

Designs like the Purple Impressions Necklace (page 18) cut the edge after beading. Always consider this when stitching the outside rows. Because these rows are created to hug the center area, it is easier to place stitches inside the planned edge and position stitches toward the center. When trimming beadwork like this, consider trimming around the beadwork, leaving space for one more row of Backstitch. After cutting, look at the back side and determine whether you can safely trim closer yet not cut any threads there. If so, trim and proceed. If there are stray stitches, simply add one more row of Backstitch on the backing, which is now a precut backing.

Neck Strand Procedures

STANDARD NECKLACE INSTRUCTIONS FOR THREAD

1 Cut 3 yards (2.7 m) of thread. Put a needle on and move it to the center to work doubled thread. Add a stop bead with a 9-inch (22.9 cm) tail.

2 Pick up one 6° bead, then pick up the beads for the necklace strand until you have the desired length for one side of the necklace.

3 Go through the bail. Depending on the type of bail you are using, add beads to sit inside the bail. Repeat step 2, in mirror image.

4 Pick up eleven 11° beads (figure 1). (Use nine for a smaller loop.) Stitch through them again to create a loop.

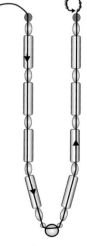

figure 1

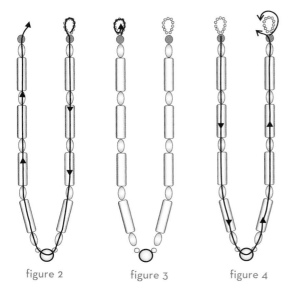

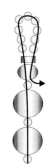

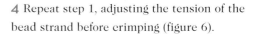

2 Pick up the beads for the necklace strand until you have the desired length for one side of the necklace.

3 Go through the bail. Depending on the type of bail you are using, add beads to sit inside the bail. Repeat step 2, in mirror image.

4 Repeat step 1, adjusting the tension of the bead strand before crimping (figure 6).

figure 6

figure 2   figure 3   figure 4

5 Stitch back through the entire strand to the starting point and remove the stop bead (figure 2). Pull all threads (there are four) to straighten and line them all up.

6 Repeat step 4, placing the loop next to the 6° bead (figure 3). Make sure you have the desired tension in the strand. Use the tail threads and needle thread and tie a square knot plus one. Add needles to the tail threads, and stitch down into the strand at least 2 inches (5.1 cm). Pull the knot into the 6° bead. Use the needle thread and stitch around the loop one more time.

7 Stitch through the entire necklace through to the 6° bead on the other side. Cut the thread near the needle, creating a tail and a needle thread. Use the needle thread and stitch around the loop (figure 4). Tie a square knot plus one using the needle and tail threads.

8 Put a needle on the tail thread and stitch down into the necklace strand at least 2 inches (5.1 cm). Pull the knot into the 6° bead. Use the needle thread and stitch around the loop one more time, then stitch down through the 6° bead and into the necklace strand at least 2 inches (5.1 cm). Cut the threads.

STANDARD NECKLACE INSTRUCTIONS FOR FLEXIBLE BEADING WIRE

1 Pick up one 6° bead, one crimp bead, and eleven 11° beads (use nine for a smaller loop). Pass back through the crimp bead and the 6° bead to create a loop (figure 5). Adjust the tension and crimp the crimp bead. Cut the tail of the wire to sit inside the 6° bead.

figure 5

STANDARD NECKLACE INSTRUCTIONS FOR DIRECT ATTACHMENT SUNSHINE EDGE—SINGLE EDGE BEAD

1 Cut 2 yards (1.8 m) of thread. Put a needle on and move it to the center to work doubled thread. Add a stop bead with a 9-inch (22.9 cm) tail.

2 Pick up one 6° bead, then pick up beads for the necklace strand until you have the desired length for one side of the necklace.

3 Stitch through the edge bead, staying on the top side, underneath the surface beadwork. Stitch through the backings to the back side at least ¼ inch (6 mm) from the edge (figure 7).

figure 7

4 Stitch out through the edge bead and through the entire bead strand. Remove the stop bead.

5 Pick up eleven 11° seed beads (use nine for a smaller loop). Stitch through them again to create a loop.

6 Adjust the tension in the bead strand. Use the tail thread and needle thread and tie a square knot plus one. Put a needle on the tail thread and stitch 2 inches (5.1 cm) down the bead strand, pulling the knot into the 6° bead. With the needle thread, stitch around the loop again and then down through the bead strand.

7 Repeat step 3. Cut the thread near the needle, creating two threads. Make a small stitch through the backings with one of the threads. Use the threads to tie a square knot. Weave in the threads and cut.

STANDARD NECKLACE INSTRUCTIONS FOR DIRECT ATTACHMENT SUNSHINE EDGE—TWO EDGE BEADS

1 Cut 2 yards (1.8 m) of thread. Put a needle on and move it to the center to work doubled thread. Add a stop bead with a 9-inch (22.9 cm) tail.

2 Pick up one 6° bead, then pick up beads for the necklace strand until you have the desired length for one side of the necklace.

3 Pick up three to five 11° beads. Stitch through one of the selected edge beads, staying on the back side. Stitch through the backings to the top side at least ¼ inch (6 mm) from the edge (figure 8). Position the needle over to the other edge bead, staying under the surface beadwork (figure 9). Stitch through the backings to the back side at least ¼ inch (6 mm) from the edge.

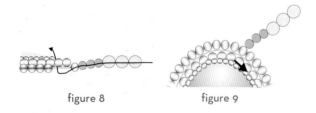

figure 8   figure 9

4 Stitch out through the edge bead. Pick up three to five 11° beads and stitch through the entire bead strand (figure 10). Remove the stop bead.

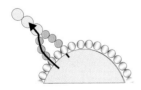

figure 10

5 Pick up eleven 11° beads (use nine for a smaller loop). Stitch through them again to create a loop.

6 Adjust the tension in the bead strand. Use the tail thread and needle thread and tie a square knot plus one. Put a needle on the tail thread and stitch 2 inches (5.1 cm) down the into bead strand, pulling the knot into the 6° bead. With the needle thread, stitch around the loop again and then down through the entire bead strand.

7 Stitch through the added seed beads on one side and through the edge bead, staying on the top side. Stitch through the backings to the back side under the beadwork at least ¼ inch (6 mm) from the edge (figure 11). Stitch up through the edge bead, the added seed beads above it, and the added beads on the other side, and then down through the edge bead, staying on the front side (figure 12). Stitch through to the back side under the beadwork at least ¼ inch (6 mm) from the edge. Cut the thread near the needle, creating two threads. Make a small stitch through the backings with one of the threads. Use the threads to tie a square knot. Weave in the threads and cut.

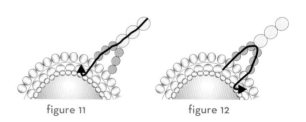

figure 11   figure 12

STANDARD NECKLACE INSTRUCTIONS FOR DIRECT ATTACHMENT CLEAN EDGE

1 Cut 2 yards (1.8 m) of thread. Put a needle on and move it to the center to work doubled thread. Add a stop bead with a 9-inch (22.9 cm) tail.

2 Pick up one 6° bead, then pick up beads for the necklace strand until you have the desired length for one side of the necklace.

3 Pick up three to five 11° beads. Stitch up through the top edge bead (figure 13). From the back side, stitch through the backings to the top side at least ¼ inch (6 mm) from the edge. Stitch over to the other edge bead using the Running Stitch and though the backings to the back side at least ¼ inch (6 mm) from the edge on the far side of the other edge bead. Stitch up through the edge bead and pick up three to five 11° beads. Stitch through the entire bead strand (figure 14). Remove the stop bead.

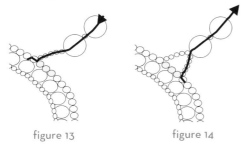

figure 13   figure 14

4 Pick up eleven 11° beads (use nine for a smaller loop). Stitch through them again to create a loop. Adjust the tension in the bead strand. Use the tail thread and needle thread and tie a square knot plus one. Put a needle on the tail thread and stitch 2 inches (5.1 cm) down into the bead strand, pulling the knot into the 6° bead. With the needle thread, stitch around the loop again and then down through the bead strand.

5 Stitch through the added seed beads on the top and up through the edge bead, staying on the front side (figure 15). Stitch through the backings to the back side under the beadwork at least ¼ inch (6 mm) from the edge. Stitch through the edge bead, through the added seed beads over to the other side, through those added seed beads, and down through the edge bead, staying on the front side (figure 16). Stitch through to the back side under the beadwork at least ¼ inch (6 mm) from the edge. Cut the thread near the needle, creating two threads. Make a small stitch through the backings with one of the threads. Use the threads to tie a square knot. Weave in the threads and cut.

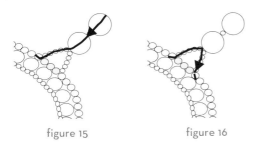

figure 15   figure 16

Techniques Index

I've created this index to help you identify the stitches and techniques referred to in the project instructions. Often in beading the same stitch is known by more than one name; however, the illustrations that follow will resolve that problem. If you encounter a technique that you are not familiar with, you can substitute with one that you do know to create your own unique design. You may also want to refer to my books Beading with Cabochons and Dimensional Bead Embroidery for a comprehensive review of how to do the stitches and techniques.

COMBINING

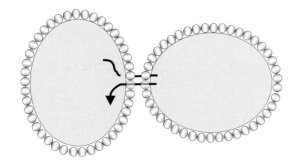

Combining joins separate pieces of bead embroidery (components). Stitch through the Sunshine Edge beads and through the backings. Pieces can be joined directly edge to edge, or beads can be stitched in between.

SURFACE STITCHES

BACKSTITCH

Backstitch is the most-often-used stitch in bead embroidery. All types will produce a row of beads. You can select one type and use it all the time, or use them all depending on the situation. When beading around a focal, use the 4-6 Backstitch and the 4-2 Backstitch (figures 1 and 2) because they are faster and the focal holds the shape of the line even for tight curves. When beading on an open area, use the 2-3 Backstitch (figure 3) because it is a tighter stitch. You can switch from one to another even in the same row of beads with no discernible effect on the beadwork.

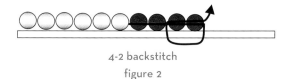

4-6 backstitch

figure 1

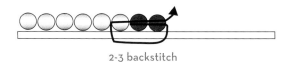

4-2 backstitch

figure 2

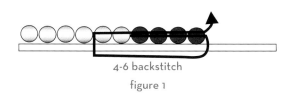

2-3 backstitch

figure 3

CLOVER STITCH

COUCH STITCH

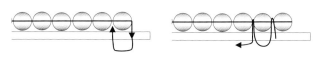

LAZY STITCH

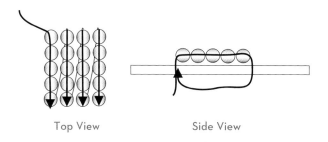

Top View   Side View

LOOP STITCH

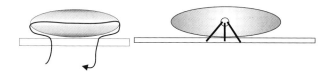

ONE-BEAD STITCH

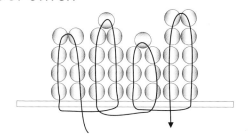

PICOT STITCH (A.K.A. MOSS STITCH)

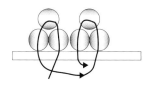

STACKS STITCH (A.K.A. FRINGE STITCH)

Turn Bead

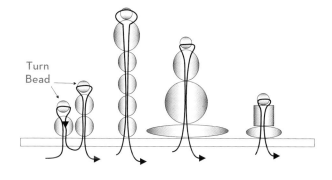

BEZEL STITCHES

BEAD-ACROSS BEZEL

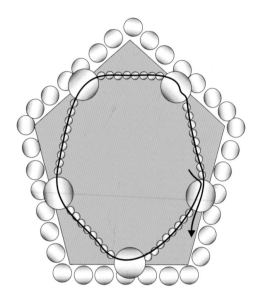

BUGLE ROW BEZEL

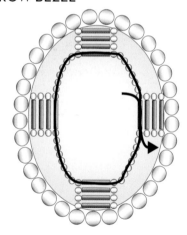

FLOWER BEZEL

STANDARD/PLAIN BEZEL

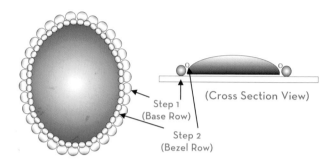

Step 1
(Base Row)

Step 2
(Bezel Row)

(Cross Section View)

The first row stitched is the base row. This is a critical row because it determines the elevation of the bezel row. The bezel row needs to be positioned upward and inward onto the surface of the focal so that the bezel row is smaller than the outside edge of the focal. For a focal that is a regular domed cabochon, an 11° bead is usually sufficient for a base row; use a larger size bead for the base row on thick-cut cabochons in order to raise the bezel row as required. Use Backstitch or Couch Stitch to create the base row. Once the row is complete, stitch around it again (through the beads only) numerous times to fill the bead holes with thread to straighten the row and strengthen it. The bezel row is stitched second and sits inside the base row, stitched on with Backstitch. Stitch around the row (through the beads only) numerous times to fill the bead holes with thread to straighten the row and strengthen it. Often there are additional rows. These are stitched around the base row using Backstitch.

This technique is often used solely for design purposes, for instance around a bead that is sewn on. In that case, the size of the base row bead, and therefore the position of the bezel row, is simply the designer's choice.

STACKS BEZEL

CIRCLES EDGE

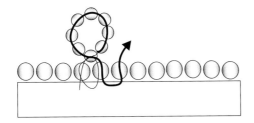

CLEAN EDGE

FRINGE EDGES

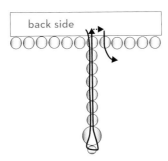

Standard Fringe

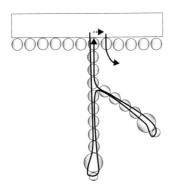

Branch Fringe

Loop Fringe

LACE RUFFLE EDGE

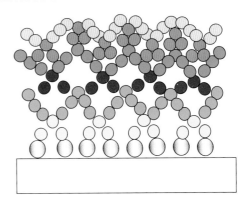

LAZY EDGE

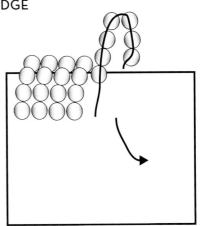

POINTED EDGE

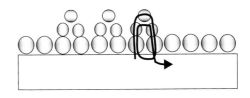

ROPE EDGE

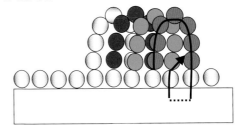

ROPE EDGE—MIDDLE BEAD VARIATION

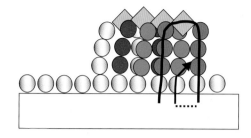

SUNSHINE EDGE—PICOT VARIATION

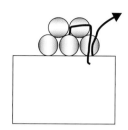

SIDE PETAL EDGE

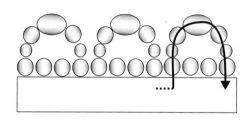

TURN BEAD EDGE

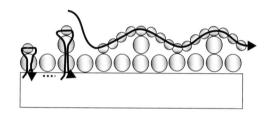

WAVE EDGE

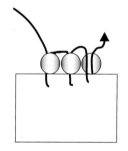

SUNSHINE EDGE (A.K.A. BASIC EDGE, RAW EDGE, OR BRICK STITCH EDGE)

OTHER STITCHES

RUNNING STITCH

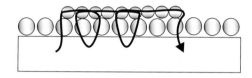

WHIPSTITCH

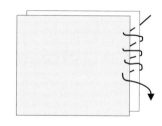
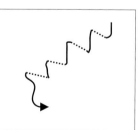

tip

Do not begin the edge by wrapping the thread around the first bead. The exposed thread is unattractive and can cause problems later if the exposed thread is cut or becomes worn. Instead, stitch through the backings to create a temporary loop to hold the thread tension, then stitch as directed above. Remove the temporary loop to finish.

ATTACHMENTS

ADDED BEAD ATTACHMENT

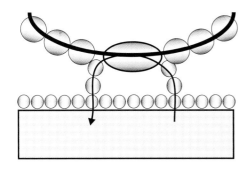

DIRECT ATTACHMENT

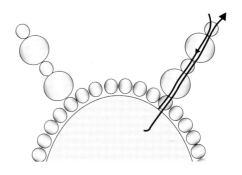

BACK SIDE BEAD ATTACHMENT

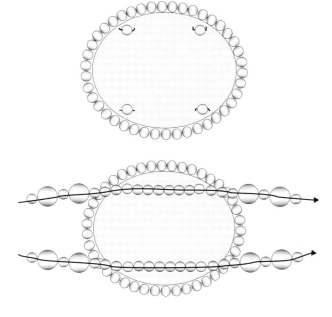

HERRINGBONE LOOP ATTACHMENT

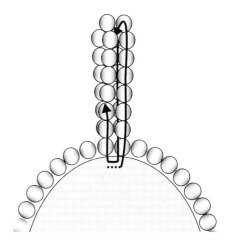

DOUBLE HERRINGBONE LOOP ATTACHMENT—SIDEWAYS LOOP VARIATION

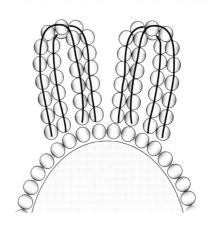

SQUARE STITCH BAIL ATTACHMENT

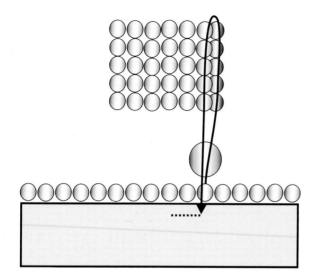

TOP LOOP ATTACHMENT

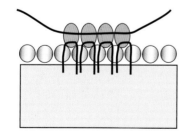

TURN BEAD ATTACHMENT

ONE-THREAD KNOT

SQUARE KNOT

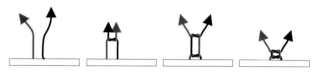

SQUARE KNOT PLUS ONE

Arline Lewis
Untitled, *2012*
Lampwork glass cabochon by Linda Sharpsteen, pearls, seed beads

Lolita J. McNesby-Gutierrez
Conversational, 2012
Agate, pearls, sterling silver, black onyx, seed beads

Pam Killingsworth
Seasons, 2012
Lampwork glass cabochons by Pam Killingsworth, Czech glass beads, seed beads

Sis Morris
Sea Her Play, 2012
Lampwork glass mermaid by Bill Irvine, pearls, metal, sea glass, ceramic, seed beads

Sis Morris
Moroccan Night, 2012
Agate, carnelian, yellow calcite, red aventurine, seed beads

Yvonne Cabalona
In the Pink!, 2012
Impression jasper, Swarovski pearls, seed beads

Sis Morris
Untitled, 2012
Chrysanthemum stone, pearls, bugle beads, seed beads

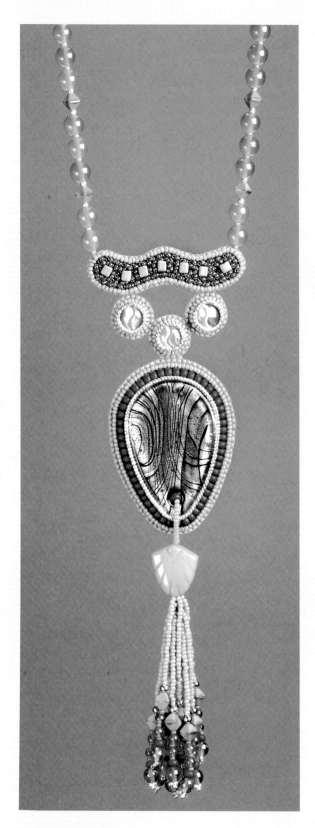

Jamie Cloud Eakin
Playin' in Spring, 2012
Foil glass pendant, snake eye cabochons, Czech glass beads, seed
beads snake eye cabochons, Czech glass beads, seed beads

About the Author

Jamie Cloud Eakin has been a professional bead artist for almost two decades, and she teaches and sells her work in galleries across North America. She is the author of *Beading with Cabochons* (Lark 2005), *Bugle Bead Bonanza* (Lark 2010), and *Dimensional Bead Embroidery* (Lark 2011). Jamie lives in Modesto, California. Her website is www.StudioJamie.com.

PHOTO BY McLEAN DESIGN

Acknowledgments

This book is dedicated to the designer and creator in all of us. I hope I have helped plant those seeds so you can nurture them and grow to your full design potential.

I want to thank my sister in life and in design, Candace, and of course my husband, Stephen, for his encouragement and patience. Thank you also to the folks at Lark, especially Kathy Sheldon for negotiating the bumps in the road and keeping things on track.

Credits

Editor
Kathy Sheldon

Art Director
Carol Barnao

Photographers
Stewart O'Shields
Jamie Cloud Eakin

Cover Designer
Carol Barnao

Editorial Assistant
Dawn Dillingham

Art Intern
Shao Khang

Index